labor love & liberation
liberation
the yoga way to birth

tina lilly

Labor, Love, and Liberation

THE YOGA WAY TO BIRTH

a guide to mindfulness and other useful disciplines
for a life-changing event

TINA LILLY

Wild Stillness Publishing
Portland, Oregon

Cover and graphic design by Gabe Decker
Book design and editing by Mark Alan Lilly

ISBN: 978-0989174114
First Published: June, 2017
yogawaytobirth.com

Please Note

This book contains suggestions for yoga practice and labor management that include physical activity, body movements and postures. They do not substitute for advice from medical professionals such as your midwife, obstetrician or primary care physician, or for exercising your own judgment.

By using any of these suggestions during your pregnancy or labor, you do so of your own free will and at your own risk. The author, publisher and the Yoga Way to Birth assume no liability or responsibility for any complications that may arise during your pregnancy or labor.

To All Love,

and my children

Contents

INTRODUCTION

I am a fortunate woman. Many years ago, by the grace of seekers before me and a humming drive for knowledge and insight within myself, I was introduced to yoga. I began a steady study and practice of this ancient discipline, and eventually acquired my credentials as a teacher.

But being a yoga teacher is not what makes me a fortunate woman. In fact, as my esteemed friend and teacher Casey Palmer humbly noted, there is no such thing as a yoga teacher. Yoga can't be taught, he says. One can only teach a method. Which is why I am a fortunate woman. I have found a method that helps me go through life with awareness, courage, and purpose.

The need for a method with such far reaching power becomes particularly important when we face big challenges or life transitions. Childbirth is one such challenge, followed by another, often greater challenge: motherhood. My good fortune was to discover yoga when I was first pregnant. I was eager to learn, eager to merge with a sea of wisdom prepared for me by generations of mothers before me. I took the plunge.

The first prenatal classes I attended gave me community, relief from pregnancy-related physical discomforts, and a break from anxiety-driven consumption of literature about what to expect when you are expecting. Yoga expanded the margins of my vision. I started to see things, about myself and about life, I hadn't seen before. It was as if I was talking directly to the source from which all experience springs. I was in communion with my body. This book is about that communion.

It is also about what I learned during my pregnancies, birth and motherhood, and about the lessons my body taught me when I was not listening. I will admit, they were hard lessons. You can read about those in detail later on but here they are in essence:

1. The degree of pain mothers experience in labor and birth correlates to the degree of which they are in honest communication with themselves and their bodies.
2. Pain is often a disguise of fear and best met with courage and kindness.

3. Pregnancy, birth, and motherhood are invitations to learn about ourselves. Refusing to accept this invitation can be costly.

4. Book learning is not enough. Mindful, direct experience of the body goes a long way.

5. Our bodies' needs aren't optional; ignoring them doesn't make them go away.

6. Attentiveness and practice are the foundations for a healthy relationship with our bodies.

7. Regular practice is mandatory.

As a new mother, I had no idea that these were valuable things to learn. I knew I had a lot to learn, but not this. I thought it was important to learn how to cook with a baby on the hip, how to soothe a crying child while talking on the phone, or how to fold piles of laundry amidst litters of toys and constant interruptions. But the real lessons were not about housekeeping or managing my baby's schedule. They were about accepting the wild and messy ride of birth and motherhood, and about learning how to keep from throwing a tantrum right along with a screaming toddler. They were about learning to slow down and how to pay attention to my inner world.

Now let me say this: I've always been a good student. I take learning seriously and do not shy away from a good challenge. Socrates once said that the unexamined life is not worth living. I'd like to expand his famous statement: The unclaimed story is not worth telling. I examined my life to hell and back and have returned with a story. It's a story worth telling, I believe, because it is embedded in larger teachings. First and foremost these are the teachings of yoga. To these I bow. I also bow to the teachings of the Buddha, and I bow to the teachings of birth.

After I gave birth to my first child, a son, I had two more children, my daughters. Each of their births was magnificent and earth-shattering in their own way and led me to teach what I learned in the tight embrace of two lovers: yoga and birth. A method was born out of this embrace: the Yoga Way to Birth.

I have been teaching the Yoga Way to Birth, a sixteen hour childbirth preparation course, in my hometown Portland, Oregon, for many years now. Hundreds of pregnant couples have taken the class since its inception in 2005. They have learned some useful, practical information about childbirth and helpful meditation practices for labor. They have listened to their beliefs, fears and desires, and they have listened to their bodies. They have stretched, moved and aimed for an enduring connection with their breath and with the power that brings it forth. It is my hope that they have also learned a thing or two about themselves and found inspiration in the process.

Inquiry into who we are and into the mysteries that govern our world and our place in it is a central part of yoga. It is also a central part of this book. To encourage your own reflections, I have tried to carry through the voice of seeker and storyteller in the writing. Give yourself time to read and feel the stories. Notice what they may bring up in you. Use them as an invitation to meditate, connect with your baby, and enter into your own place of inquiry. I extend a similar invitation when the teacher within me takes a turn and the narrative gives way to practical instructions.

For me, self-inquiry has led to teaching – which is why you will hear the didactic voice of the teacher as well. I have indicated, as well as I could, when to expect more practical advice. But the borders between inquiry and teaching are often fluid. The voices of seeker, storyteller and teacher start to blend like the melodies of a song; they go hand in hand. I hope you follow me into these terrains with curiosity and earnestness.

Beginning

How good – to be alive!
How infinite – to be
Alive, two-fold, the Birth I had
And this, besides, in Thee!

~Emily Dickinson

LESSONS IN LISTENING

This book started years ago as a seed in my womb. It was conceived long before I wrote the first page or knew what this book would be about. I was pregnant with my first baby, a boy who would arrive in the year of the Ox with the first tulips of spring, sometime in the month of Taurus. Enjoying the leisurely honeymoon of a young pregnant couple, my husband and I were looking forward to meeting our eight-hoofed little Ox, swapping anecdotes and horoscopes about the Taurus-born, especially when May rolled around, and the little bull kept us waiting. During the ten long days that stretched past his due date we joked about the stubbornness of Taurus, reminding ourselves that our son was of the kind who don't like to be rushed — which is exactly what his mother needed to learn while waiting for labor to begin.

I wish I could tell you that I waited patiently, but I did not. Instead, I researched and exercised ways to induce labor, and sought answers to my dilemma on the internet and in books. Which is exactly what I had done throughout my entire pregnancy.

Like many first-time moms, I read everything about pregnancy and birth I could get my hands on. I imagine you feel similar as your belly is getting bigger, and birth is becoming more of a reality. I spent hours browsing libraries and bookstores, and more hours reading what I could find about labor, postpartum and baby care. I was happy with what I found, anticipating with contented satisfaction the Big Day. I believed in the authority of books, and saw no reason to question what I had read. There was so much good information! I learned about the stages of birth, about the difference between early and active labor, about how to breathe, and what positions to use to ease labor pain. The more I read, the more comfortable and confident I became. Each page I turned became a seal of insurance, delivering me from ignorance to knowledge, and from knowledge, I was sure, to blissful birth.

As it turned out, I got the piece about ignorance right. I dabbled in knowledge. However, the leap from knowledge to bliss didn't happen. What I learned about birth got me as close to bliss as the memorizing of spelling words makes a good novel. It got me nowhere. When the contractions became real, I was lost. Nothing had prepared me for this. Not the books, not the birth class I faithfully took with my husband, not the visits with my doctor, and not the yoga classes I had just started taking. Labor was terrible and bewildering. Coming out of it, I wondered what had gone wrong. Had I read the wrong books? Too few, too many? Should I have taken a different childbirth class? Gone to yoga more often?

I did not think so. I had done all the right things, and yet, had missed an important piece: myself.

Each woman brings herself to birth. Like the baby who needs to descend through her womb to be born, each woman needs to descend into the depths of her own truths to be born a mother. This is often a gradual process and one with many unknowns. It requires time and radical honesty. Engaging this process has become my passion as a mother, yoga student, birth educator, and counselor. It is my touch stone. How can self-knowledge serve us, and what do we need to know about ourselves on the threshold of a new life chapter? What stands in the way?

Pregnancy is a fertile time to ask those questions, and I wished I would have asked them. Or someone else did. There were opportunities during visits with my doctor and my doula and during the birth classes my husband and I were taking, all of them missed.

For my first birth, I hired a doula. A young mother herself, Ashley (name changed) was training to become a doula. She was a large African American woman, younger than myself. Though she was skillful and caring, I did not hire her for this. I hired her because I wanted to support *her* (though this I didn't realize until later). As a white upper middle class woman, I felt responsible for giving Ashley a chance. I also wanted to feel good about myself. However, my charitable motivations didn't hold up in labor. I could not accept Ashley supporting me. My husband was equally helpless. I had not been aware of my ulterior motives when I'd decided to work with Ashley, and until I went into labor, I had little reason to question them. But missing this blind spot didn't make the truth less powerful, or painful.

Other unexamined truths affected my first birth experience as well. Tucked away in more conspicuous places of my self, it took birth to bring them to light. Unlike pregnancy which let me make excuses and dawdle, birth did not allow me the luxury of ignorance. Birth sent me to boot camp and asked everything of me, everything I knew and everything I didn't. And how little I knew.

When it was over, I felt miserable about my birth experience. I remember returning to my prenatal yoga class to tell my birth story as happened every once in a while when new moms visited with babes in arms to share words of wisdom with their still-pregnant friends. I had wanted to be one of those "wise women". Tell my eager sisters how to get through to the other side. Now I was on the other side, but I had nothing worth saying. Still, I went back to talk about my birth. I wanted to see, at the least, the awe on the faces of the pregnant moms beholding a new mother with her baby. Which is just what I had done every time when I, still with baby on the inside, saw a mother holding her newborn. Wow. Look at her. She did it.

I don't remember what story I told everyone, but it didn't matter. I got the looks I had hoped for. I was official. But after coming home, the glow faded. The doubts had never left. I was just another woman making it through birth. Here was one of the biggest events in my life, the birth of my first child, but beyond that, there was not much to say. My labor had been terrible. End of story.

The agony of my questions and the lack of answers drove me back to recall, over and over again, the hours of my son's labor. I have a photograph of myself taken shortly after his birth. I am looking into the camera with a mixture of relief and bewilderment. Here I am, holding my little baby to my breast, feeling like the survivor of a natural disaster, and knowing deep within me that this birth wasn't over. In the months and years that followed, I walked the way to my son's birth back in time, soul-searching, asking questions. I had to understand what had happened. I had to understand what the pain had been all about, what birth was all about, and what I had to do with it. I bowed to the woman I wished I had been in labor, and embraced the woman I ended up being. Together we began retrieving soul-piece after soul-piece of this difficult and rich experience.

WHY I WROTE THIS BOOK

I wrote this book because I want to share those lessons with you. I learned the hard way how to open in labor, as do many first-time moms, and telling my stories may help you have an easier birth.

One of the biggest take-aways from my trials in birth and postpartum was this: my body matters. It has a voice worth listening to and is worthy of my attention and care. It deserves to be treated well. But not only for my own sake, or during the hours of labor. I believe that the health of our individual bodies is intrinsically connected to the health of our planet. How we treat our bodies says a lot about how we relate to planet Earth.

I believe future generations need us to be knowledgeable and loving towards our bodies. Treating your body with respect and kindness is not just a good idea because you want to have a healthy baby and stay healthy yourself, but because the future of the next generations depends on it. I hope:

- That we, as birthing mothers, increase our awareness and appreciation of the body as a guide to wellness, integrity and power (in childbirth and in life).
- That we, as birthing mothers, claim the power and mystery of childbirth as our inheritance.
- That we, as birthing mothers, continue to return to where we have found strength and wisdom for centuries – home in our bodies, home on Mother Earth.

I admit: This is an ambitious undertaking and the grand, cosmic vision of this book. Let us be mindful of our bodies to make a healthy home for our children and grandchildren. Let us fill our minds with the rich narrative of our physical selves – arms, ears, belly, joints, brain and all. Let us live in all of our senses, not just in our heads. Let us embody birth.

I also wrote this book because I love yoga and how it helped me so deeply in the births of my children. I want to share this love with you, and I want you to have the most amazing birth possible. I want to encourage and support you to be daring. Take heart to learn about yourself with the same fervor as learning about the phases of labor or the best food for newborns. Keep taking responsibility. Keep falling in love with your body, deeply, and care for it with diligence and passion. Your body is sacred ground.

WHO THIS BOOK IS FOR

This book is for pregnant women and mothers who want to learn about birth through wakeful engagement with their body and mind. If you are looking for comprehensive information about the birth process, labor positions, medical options and partner support, it may not be the book you are looking for (check Further Reading for recommendations).

The primary focus of this book is inspiration, not information. Information can be comforting as it helps us to know what to expect, especially when we go into situations we have never been in before. But regardless of how much information we gather, at the end of the day we are left with ourselves, our habitual patterns, learned responses and deep unconscious beliefs. Much of what I picked up during my first pregnancy in the classes I took and in the books I read, though comprehensive and well presented, didn't serve me in the throes of labor and birth. I couldn't access the part of my brain where this information was stored. The details of timing, dilation, hormones and positioning were useful really only later on – in helping me to fill in the narrative gaps of my birth stories. The more important and effective kind of knowledge is well-applied self-knowledge. The Buddha once noted we don't have control over circumstances, only over our responses and actions. Self-knowledge and honest inquiry into who we are fosters this ability.

So if you are ready to follow and trust your inner experiences, you and I are on the same path. But be prepared. This is not necessarily an easy path. It is the path of a warrior.

When you open yourself up to experience, you don't always come up with pleasant pieces. You may encounter painful sensations, nasty thoughts, uncomfortable emotions, and difficult memories, and be tempted to push them away. But if you can tolerate potential temporary discomfort and stay with your experience, you may find the answers you were looking for. Answers are the offspring of experience, discernment and reflection. Like stretch marks on the belly, they are earned after the fact and yours to keep.

This warrior path is for anyone willing to walk it – which is why I am offering this book also to the partners, loved ones, friends, doulas and midwives who support a mother in labor. These practices work! The transformative power of yoga has not been lost on anyone who earnestly tried it. This does not mean that they will guarantee an easy birth. Birth is not a math equation with a predictable answer. Yoga works because it changes you from the inside out.

WHAT TO EXPECT

When I came up with the title of this book (watching a dance performance of my oldest daughter), I couldn't help but smile: All three words start with the letter "L", just like the last name of my three children, the Lilly kids. This book is about them and what their births have taught me about labor, love and liberation.

I wish I could say that I started my journey to motherhood with Love. Not that I didn't love becoming (and being) pregnant and preparing for birth, but my love was fickle. I did not endure when labor demanded Love full force. So my stories must start with Labor and the body's trials and pains.

In German (my native language), the word for "labor" (as it relates to childbirth) is "Wehe". It's a word every German child learns at a very young age but not because German children are particularly interested in childbirth. It becomes part of their first vocabulary because "Wehe" means pain or potential pain. German parents use this word, often accompanied by a stern face and a wagging finger, when their children misbehave and need to be reminded that their behavior will have consequences unless they do as Mom or Dad say. Which is exactly what happened to me on the threshold to motherhood. Birth wagged her mighty finger because I wanted to have things my way, and labor hurt. A lot.

I will talk about my understanding of "Birth" in detail in Part Two of this book, *Coming to Terms*. Here I will explain some of my word choices and important concepts of this book. It also introduces the Yoga Way to Birth, a childbirth preparation program I have been developing and teaching in Portland, Oregon, for the past decade.

Part Three, *Labor*, is divided into two sections. The first section shares my birth experiences and introduces six facets of birth: Birth is primal, truthful, wise, wild, patient and beautiful. These facets are the parting gifts of my labors and the foundation for a relational model of birth and birth education (which I will explain in detail later on). They have helped me better understand who I am and who I am not, and what birth is and is not.

The second half of Part Three covers basic information about the process of labor, and includes meditations on breathing, practice suggestions and questions for self-reflection. Please supplement this information with other reading if you are hungry for more (see Further Reading for recommendations).

Part Four, *Love*, reflects on the nature of body and mind, and how to be in loving relationship with both. Giving birth to a child is a divine event, reverberating the same vibratory force that gave rise to the cosmos. In Hindu mythology, this force is God Shiva, the Eternal Absolute. Before the beginning of time, Shiva sits on top of the Himalayas, absorbed in deep meditation until Parvati, incarnation of the Divine feminine power Shakti, rouses him from his sleep. From their desire for each other and from the Divine Love of their union the universe is born. All is made of this Love – atoms, particles, rays, magnetic fields, liquids, solids, solar systems, mind, body, you, and me.

But we easily forget. Often, we get carried away by our minds, lost in our desires and egos, ignorant of our bodies. Human nature is, by default, conditional. Having a body and a mind gives rise to contingencies, apparent causes, obvious effects and assumed responsibilities. The gravitational force of our thoughts, sensations and desires is so compelling that we often do little else, experience little else, and expect little else on any given day. We forget to love. We forget to surrender.

Part Four investigates how to return to Love, even when the body is "failing" us in labor, or our mind tries to make us believe the shadows. It builds a case for the practice of yoga and mindfulness which is discussed in detail in the last part of this book.

Part Five, *Liberation*, highlights yoga as a practical and effective discipline for embracing labor, and for returning to Love. It discusses the foundations of yoga, and includes meditations, more stories, and inspirations for practice. They are based on the following beliefs:

1. I have a body.
2. My body was born and will not last forever.
3. I have a mind that reflects my body's condition.
4. The same mind is capable of reflecting the unconditional and unconditioned Truth.
5. I am not my body and mind.
6. I am Love.

Part Six, *Formal Practice*, concludes with specific guidelines and suggestions for meditation and asana practice. Regular and diligent practice is of great importance if you want your labor to be most loving and liberating. Whether this takes the form of meditation, asana (yoga postures), pranayama (breathing), devotional chanting, self-less service, reading spiritual texts, or practicing kindness and compassion doesn't matter. As the Persian poet Rumi said, "There are hundreds of ways to kneel and kiss the ground."

Coming to Terms

Capable Amazing Sensitive Intelligent
Mind Changeable Uncomfortable Sturdy
Vessel Mine Grounded Glad
Strong Water Heavy
Growing House Ripe Powerful
Experience Round Impediment
Imperfect Transitioning
Abundant Roots
Unified Endure Home Love

~Yoga Way to Birth class participants about the body

Words are powerful. They are like seeds, potent little powerhouses capable of creating universes. As a writer, they are my tools. As an educator, they are my responsibility. I exercised care when I wrote this book because what I say and how I say it can affect you and your birth experience. This chapter explains the most important concepts in holistic birth education and what they mean to me. This being said, you don't need to agree with me. Consider my definitions an invitation to explore more deeply what you believe and what not. Make up your own words and meaning, for they are the most powerful.

BIRTH

What is birth like? What will labor feel like in my body?

These and many other questions went through my mind when I was first pregnant, as they probably sit with you as well holding this book. I had my ideas about birth, carefully assembled and cherished as my belly grew bigger.

I sensed birth would be a life-changing event, something akin to a major test that would decide my future, and with earnest zeal I set out to prepare for the big day. I did what I knew how to do well: buckled up, opened my text books, and studied. I learned my ABC's and all about Apgar, Beta strep and Crowning. I started taking a yoga class, went swimming two times a week, and signed my husband and me up for a Bradley childbirth class with a local midwife. I was the perfect student, and was sure I would get all the answers right when the sacred hush of birth would fall upon me. But when it did, the lights went out. Birth appeared unlike anything I'd expected, pushing my smart consultations into her shadow.

Birth was a lot bigger than I had thought. She was majestic! Being in labor was humbling, which is one of the reasons why I capitalize the word *Birth* (unless I talk about childbirth in general, in which case I keep the lower case). It is as an expression of my respect for the power of Birth and a way to emphasize its relational nature.

Birth brings you into direct relationship with yourself (with your body, thoughts, emotions, desires, memories, fears, beliefs etc), whether you want to or not. Relationship is about communication and contact, and contact is the mother of experience. How you make contact (with your body, thoughts, emotions, desires, memories, fears, beliefs etc) can define how you go through labor and give birth.

My first contact with Birth was overly confident followed by shock and surprise followed by fear followed by helpless surrender. Labor was a painful process of *unlearning*. Let's get things right, Birth said, and stripped off my coats and turned out my pockets until nothing was left but me. Naked, belly-bursting me. Now let me show you how to have this baby, she urged. Let's start here, for this you need to know: Birth is not about you, and is all about you.

This was her heaving message: *Know yourself, and then let it go. In this, you will find me. You will realize you can do anything. There will be no space where you can't go, no passage too narrow or too dark to cross. Be. Here. With. Me. Now.*

This may sound like a big undertaking, but it's actually quite simple. All you need to do is start with one deep breath.

Take one, and open wide the door to awareness. Learn about yourself, ask questions, and don't take no for an answer. Listen with your mind, body and heart.

Take two, and connect with the rhythm of Birth: The womb contracts, the womb relaxes, the womb rests. Repeat, until baby is born. Persevere. This is how it is done.

Birth wants you to understand her. Your steady companion since you became pregnant, Birth has been walking next to you, reminding you that this is the holy work of mothers: conceiving, nurturing, and letting go. But Birth is not casual about her teachings. As the supreme ruler of new beginnings, Birth assumes full authority when it is her time to initiate life-altering changes of renewal and growth. Birth divides and separates: flower petal from bud, root from seed, fetus from womb. This separation is powerful beyond measure. Seed pods need to break open, bodies shift and rearrange. For human mothers, Birth's command extends to the ego and mind. These too need to open and align in service. Yoga offers a perfect framework for learning how to do just that.

YOGA

Most people in the U.S. think of postures, meditation and breathing exercises when they hear the word yoga. I was one of them, many years back. But yoga is a lot more than a set of exercises.

Quantum theory holds that light can both be a particle and a wave. It is neither nor, and dependent on the presence of the observer. Yoga can be defined similarly: as both an action (wave) and a particular state (particle). Here is a short-hand definition. Yoga is:

1. a series of spiritual practices that involve the body in mindful inquiry and

2. a state of being and seeing.

The state of yoga is often described as union, or, as T.K.V. Desikachar put it, "attainment of something previously unattainable"[1]. It begins with arriving. There are many ways to arrive. You can arrive at the yoga studio where you roll out your yoga mat, arrive on a meditation cushion, or arrive right now in this moment while holding this book.

In either situation, you have chosen to change your way of being through alteration of awareness. Conscious choice here is key. When you consciously choose to get off the roller coaster of your daily agendas, when you slow down and pause to become aware of yourself as manifest in body, emotion and thought, you practice yoga *and* arrive in its abode. You see and become the seer.

This arriving can be as transient as one breath, or it can be an enduring state of self-realization. How long it lasts depends on the degree of your repeated effort to open the portal of presence. There are various practices to support this effort, discovered and developed by seekers in India over the past five thousand years. Over the centuries, these practices have given rise to different schools and traditions. Some of the main traditions are Raja yoga, Hatha yoga, Karma yoga, Bhakti yoga and Jnana yoga.

In Hatha yoga, which is where my yoga roots are, practices are centered on the body as an object of inquiry and vehicle for spiritual fulfillment. The most popular and widely practiced Hatha yoga methods in the U.S. include postures, breathing practices and meditation. Less known are the ethical and philosophical underpinnings of yoga. In the tradition of Raja yoga they are called yamas and niyamas. In Part Five, *Liberation*, I will cover them in more detail.

The late yoga master B.K.S. Iyengar compared the yamas and niyamas to the roots of a tree from which six other limbs grow: asana (postures), pranayama (breathing exercises), pratyahara, dharana, dhyana (three progressive states of meditation) and samadhi (continuous, uninterrupted merging with divine consciousness). Together, those eight limbs make up the royal path of Raja yoga.

---

1 T.K.V. Desikachar, *The Heart of Yoga* (Rochester: Inner Traditions International, 1999) 5.

MINDFULNESS

Mindfulness is a state of non-judgmental awareness of your body sensations, functions, thoughts, feelings, or of consciousness itself. It is the capacity to notice and witness presently occurring experiences without attachment. As such, mindfulness is an expression of a yogic mind.

BODY MIND

Body and mind are manifestations of consciousness. While they are often discussed as distinct entities, their separation is arbitrary. Mind and body exist on the same continuum. Like two sides of the same coin they are interdependent, coexisting representations of consciousness.

Consciousness of mind manifests as mental faculty capable of perception, thought, memory, emotion, will, imagination, reason and cognitive functions.

Consciousness of body manifests as sensory faculty capable of perception, memory, emotion, will and physiological functions. Both body and mind receive and process information based on their interaction with the world. The result of this process is subjective experience.

Yoga has a useful model for understanding the mind-body continuum, called *koshas*. According to Hindu philosophy, human beings are composed of five "sheaths" or koshas. Interconnected and progressively subtle, the koshas advance from gross, corporeal layers to more concealed and less tangible metaphysical layers.

The first layer (anna-maya-kosha) constitutes the physical body made up of muscles, bones, organs and other physical matter. This is how we tend to define "body" in the West. The second layer (prana-maya-kosha) is the energy body. It circulates life energy (prana or breath) throughout the entire body. The third layer (mano-maya-kosha) houses what we typically refer to when we think of the mind: our thoughts, emotions, memories and ego. From here we progress to the wisdom body (vinjana-maya-kosha), the seat of discernment, conscience, intuition, witness and divine will. Consciousness of body and mind typically circulates in the first four layers, but with diligence and devotion we may enter the fifth (ananda-maya-kosha): Pure Consciousness, the abode of Jivatman, or the Divine Self.

JIVATMAN

ANANDA-MAYA-KOSHA

VIJNANA-MAYA-KOSHA

MANO-MAYA-KOSHA

PRANA-MAYA-KOSHA

ANNA-MAYA-KOSHA

CONTRACTION

Contractions are collections of energy. They pool resources and bundle forces to generate momentum for the creation of something new. Like a deep exhale, contractions aim for dormant places and add critical mass to impending transformation. They are the mandatory impulse that makes inhalation (and expansion) possible.

For this reason, I use the word contraction (versus surge or wave) to describe the work of labor. A labor contraction is the body's concentrated effort to gather maximum force and focus to birth a child. It also reflects an essential quality of the birthing mind: Single-pointed, fully awake and centered on the moment-to-moment experience of the laboring body, it aligns with the task force of Birth.

SELF & SELF

These terms capture the spectrum of human self-conscious experience and try to give meaning to who we are. When we talk about myself and yourself, we usually refer to our "smaller" self. It houses the ego (including our personal desires and the laws of the physical body and mind) and dwells primarily in the first three koshas. The small self has many names, identities and story lines. It comes into existence when we are born and dies when we take our last breath. The greater Self transcends all this. It is our un-named, timeless and indivisible soul essence and often known as Love, God, or Ātman in the yoga tradition. It resides in the wisdom and bliss body.

It is important to note that Buddhism diverts from Hinduism regarding the Self. The Buddha argued that there is no such thing as a self, Atman or God. He advocated for the idea of emptiness or no-self. Emptiness here doesn't mean the absence of anything, or that you and I don't exist. It means that the you and I or everything else for that matter have inherent nature. Nothing exists by itself or belongs to anyone or anything. This book for example doesn't belong to me, nor do the ideas or words therein. They came from a stream of collective wisdom and interdependent functions and forms. I neither own them nor do "I" have an inherent, separate existence from you, from the man that delivers my mail, or from a rain puddle or butterfly.

Both approaches to the nature of reality, the Hindu concept of Self and the Buddhist idea of no-self, can be helpful in labor. Both transcend the finite demands of ego and enable a birthing mindset that renders our fixation with our smaller self (my body, my pain etc) irrelevant.

GOD

My definition of God is a personal one, as it should be. Nothing is as personal and connected to our life experiences as our spiritual beliefs. Mine began in communist East Germany which, for the sake of finding God, was a most fortunate circumstance. While Communism is a deplorable system in regards to freedom, it gave me the freedom to find my own way to God. Because there was no God when I grew up. Religion and faith-based practices were considered outdated and hokey. God was officially, as Nietzsche had proclaimed, dead. As a child, I never visited a church (except for tourist purposes), saw a bible, or folded my hands in prayer.

Yet Communism taught me that I had to believe in something. I was groomed to prescribe to communist idealism, but life shaped my religion more than Lenin's manifesto. I found God in the silent blaze of stars on a dark and icy winter night, in the damp veins of a big fir tree felled by a mighty storm, in the booming voice of Bach's Great Fugue, in the eyes of my newborn daughter. God was everywhere if I only looked, and God was Love.

THE YOGA WAY TO BIRTH

Yoga, to me, is a perfect way to connect to this Love. I've also found it to be a perfect match for birth. Like a loving couple, yoga and birth support and complement each other while answering to a mutual call. They are twin experiences born from the same root and nurtured with the same longing: to be present in body and mind, and loving in all endeavors. But like many couples, they have their differences. Yoga is a practice. Birth is not.

As the more flexible and easygoing "partner", yoga lets me repeat what Birth can not. When I miss going to class today, I can try again tomorrow. When I am unable to accept a painful situation, I can make an effort next time around. An ongoing rehearsal of letting go into the Now, yoga lets me try again. With Birth, there is no next time. She doesn't take any chances. More radical and wild, her only time is Now. When a woman goes into labor, Birth is bidding her to follow. Open *Now. Now* let go.

To open and let go at a moment's notice is not easy, especially if you've had little experience with it. This is where yoga comes in. Yoga offers a chance to practice what you are trying to attain. It anchors your efforts in purposeful assignment and reflection. Go and try, yoga gently urges. Don't give up. Don't beat yourself up either. It's okay if you fall. Just find your way back up, in time. It's okay to go slow, but go. Keep showing up.

Which is what I tried to do as a new mom, who had no other choice. I tried to breathe when I felt like screaming. I tried to slow down when I wanted to run. And made mistakes, atoned, and tried again. It was in the moments of trying that I was born a mother. In trying, I was redeemed.

Eventually, my trials turned into small successes. These I felt compelled to share with other women and couples. I immersed myself in studies to become a prenatal yoga instructor and labor doula. Then, after teaching for several years and attending births, a good friend of mine asked me if I wanted to collaborate in developing a childbirth preparation program based on yoga. I didn't think twice. The Yoga Way to Birth was born.

While our young children played together around our kitchen tables, Deah Baird and I created the teaching curriculum and started offering classes at a local birth center. We met in our desire to teach a childbirth class that gives the body its rightful place in birth education. Deah brought her experience as a trained midwife and naturopath, and I drew from my studies of yoga and from the births I had attended. What we came up with was a blend of traditional childbirth education and contemporary body-mind practices.

Over the years, our program grew and changed. Deah moved on to dedicate herself to her new work as a professional counselor, and until new teaching partners came on board I held the reigns of teaching and program development alone. As a result, the Yoga Way to Birth increasingly reflected my personal understanding of yoga and birth – and grew into the book you are holding.

A core aspect of my understanding is that both yoga and birth are experience-based opportunities for personal learning and spiritual growth. Both yoga and birth bring you into intimate contact with your body, mind and self. This contact is a powerful foundation for learning. It is also the core aim of the Yoga Way to Birth classes which come together in the following three guiding principles:

1. Learn from your body: This is about being aware of the present as it is unfolding from moment to moment within your body, just as your body is responding to the present from moment to moment.
2. Get to know yourself better: The yogic practice of self-inquiry (Sanskrit: svadhyaya) is about inquiry into your feelings, motivations, needs, aspirations, assumptions and self.
3. Keep doing it: Personal practice is what gives momentum to your efforts. It engages the mind as a reflective audience of your body's actual, non-conceptual experience (of birth, breath, pain, pleasure etc).

Practice teaches you how to listen effectively to the narrative of your body, sharing its own story in real time. For example, when practicing a deep forward bend in yoga, you may feel a burning sensation in your hamstrings, and notice, like barnacles clinging to a rock, numerous thoughts and feelings attached to this sensation. You may compare yourself to other hamstrings, feel pleased or displeased, impatient, motivated, bored, scared; you name it. All this is great information – as long as you can hear it simply, unconditionally, and without judgment. Feeling tired? Notice it. Uncomfortable? Notice this too.

Continue to notice in this fashion everything that moves through your awareness. See the "barnacles", and how they assume the shape of the rock. Keep at it, and you start to see that they are not the rock. The rock is something entirely different. It is embodied, un-named experience, the birth place of sacred ground.

Getting to the "rock" takes patience and time. When you start to pay attention to the inner landscape of experience during yoga, you come face to face with your restless mind. Thoughts run wild, piggy-backing, playing tag, leaping and bouncing from one to another. Feeling states change in rapid succession like clouds pushed across the sky by strong winds. So be it. It is noisy in there. Wait. Be patient and insist on dimming the lights until the noise fades and a vision of silence takes hold. Insist on this vision like a new mother who nurses herself and her baby to sleep – trusting that she will sleep again through the night in due time. Hold on to this vision like the same mother who lights the candles on her child's birthday cake – knowing that the room will fall quiet when she brings in the sweet frosted treat with the glowing lights on top. Trust and continue to sit quietly, patiently waiting to extract an ounce of silence from your noisy mind:

Be   Here

Keep calling for the sweet balm of silence to flow forth from your mind like mother's milk from nursing breasts. Gently urge your mind to latch on to the source of this nourishment. Wait for the letdown. And arrive.

Labor

It's here
In the in between
Where pain becomes our infinite gift
It's our own suffering
That causes the shift
And allows the birthing pangs to begin.
It's here in the blind spot
That we realize we put ourselves where we are
And therefore we can take us back.

~J. McCurdy

Our lives are stories, and so is birth. When the birth of your baby is an event of the past, you will have a story left to tell: your birth story. What you tell and how you tell it depends on many factors: where you give birth, who is there with you, the details of your labor. But there are two main players that will give this story a unique profile: Birth and you. In due time, you will meet, and from the alchemy of this encounter a story will emerge.

This chapter contains my birth stories and how I came to know Birth. They were buried in the guts of my labors and retrieved through inquiry and self-reflection which my yoga practice afforded me over the years. In my experience, Birth is this: primal, truthful, wise, wild, patient, and beautiful. This is also what Birth needed *me* to be. Embracing each of these aspects brought me into alignment with Birth and her power. It hasn't been lost on me since.

Birth is Primal

The prime role of Birth is to bring things into being so that they may live. Whereas Pregnancy, Birth's sister, tends to this role by nourishing your body and your baby's body *as one*, Birth initiates their separation. For nine months, your baby and you are indivisible, but when the time for Birth has come, this needs to end. If it doesn't, your baby, and you, will not live. This is serious business. Birth, as the ultimate midwife, will do anything she can to deliver you and your baby safely to the shore of life. Her main goal, however, is the *baby's* survival. She doesn't care how her precious charge emerges from your body; all that matters is that it does. This may conflict with your wishes and expectations for your own birth experience. Many women wish for a natural, vaginal childbirth without drugs and other medical interventions, and often this is possible. But at other times it is not. Some babies take their first breath only after their mothers have received an epidural, been opened by vacuum extraction, forceps, or the Cesarean knife. Those babies live because their mothers have made sacrifices. They have sacrificed hopes and dreams, egos, blood, tears, and virgin tissues. Consciously or not, they have surrendered to Birth's uncompromising command that their babies *must* live.

But Birth is not a bully. As a life-affirming energy, Birth will work closely with your body to ensure safe passage of your child. Your body shares one single desire with Birth: the desire for self-preservation. This desire manifests as an ongoing effort to maintain balance by harmonizing, moment to moment, contrasting forces. Breathing in and breathing out, your living body is in a constant mode of expansion and contraction to bring opposing forces into balance. Every aspect of your physical being answers to this rhythm. This rhythm is the ancient beat of the universe, the organizing pattern of creation that energizes atoms and animates cells, bodies and ecosystems.

Expansion and contraction are the shuttles of labor. Those two processes move labor along and compose the rhythm of Birth. They give rise to each other –inhale gives rise to exhale, exhale to inhale– and they happen simultaneously. When the uterus contracts, the cervix stretches (expands); and when the uterus returns to rest (expands), the cervix contracts. If you like, you can do a short practice to observe those co-existing rhythms. Make sure you sit with a relaxed posture and straight spine. Notice how inhale and exhale fold into one another. Notice parts of your body expanding while others are contracting.

Birth abides by this rhythm. Like a conductor keeping time, she takes care that the laboring mother inhales and exhales, expands and contracts in equal measure. Both need to be present to bring forth, and sustain, life.

With my first baby, I did not breathe. Birth was a single, never-ending contraction. My uterus, my breath, my jaw, my chest – everything was in a state of contraction. Paralyzed by a pain I did not expect or knew how to handle, expansion and relief were not possible. It would have taken the courage to go toward the pain, but this I was not able to do.

With my second and third baby, I did things differently. I tried to work with my body and with the lawfulness of Birth from the beginning. Each time my uterus contracted, I followed the sensation of contractions closely, from their faint rumblings at the start, to their highest peak, to the memory of mortal embrace. This focus itself was a contraction. A singular, one-pointed, steady beam of awareness, it cast through confusion like a ray of sunlight through dark forest. Worlds came into being, vast, spacious, and ever changing. I witnessed the beginning of time.

Focus of mind delivered me to this prime place of being. This, and my breathing body. Our bodies are the narrators of our inner and outer environment, tirelessly telling the story of expansion and contraction and of everything that is happening in between. Driven by one single purpose, our bodies speak of this balancing act as if their lives depend on it. And they do! In labor, it is also the life of our babies. Contractions need to be matched with expansions to meet Birth's primal duty to life. If not, the body switches into crisis mode, and crisis is painful.

I will talk about pain more later on but let me say this: pain is a great motivator. It mobilizes us to bring about change. You can change the amount of labor pain by moving into a different position, by getting an epidural (if this is an option), or by going into the heart of the contraction. Whatever you choose, all are equally valid strategies to bring yourself and labor back into balance. They are acts of bravery and surrender. Birth is not picky about what you do, but she will demand exhale and expansion. She will urge you to make room for the child that wants to be born. She will insist that your body releases what no longer belongs, relinquishing the memory of when your baby and you were one.

BIRTH IS TRUTHFUL: FELIX'S BIRTH

My first labor taught me that Birth is truthful. Birth doesn't care much about wishful thinking, or pretend to be something she is not. Birth is utterly real and expects the same from yourself. She asks that you are truthful – truthful about your desires, fears and yourself. She wants the truth about you and what you are capable of.

When I was pregnant with my first baby I was intrigued by the idea of painless childbirth and believed that this was possible. If there were women who could have pain-free labors and orgasmic births, then I could too! I had a positive self-image, a wonderful husband, a healthy body, a doctor I loved, and trusted in a loving universe that would get me what I wanted. Sure, I had heard that labor was painful, and had seen videos of women crying out in pain, but none of it threw me off course. I dwelt in blissful ignorance.

Sure enough, when labor starts, I am confident I can handle it. Actually, I'm thrilled! I feel the contractions, rhythmically and increasingly dramatic in my lower belly, but I am on top of them. Did I not know it? If this was labor (which I believe it is as I've been having regular contractions for a couple of hours) then what was all the fuss about? Having a baby was easy, and I am doing it!

A couple more hours pass in cheerful anticipation when my husband, my doula and I decide to go to the hospital. We drive over, and check into our room in the wee hours of the night. The contractions have not let up during that transition, and keep churning in my pelvis. They begin groaning like a hungry animal that has not been fed in a long time. I'm getting nervous. What is this? Labor shouldn't hurt, but those contractions feel terrifying.

Early May morning reaches through the window blinds, and I feel tired. I have been laboring for the past eight hours with contractions coming like clockwork every four minutes. I feel something should have been happening by now. Something should be different. But all that is happening is contraction after contraction after contraction. I call for a pelvic exam. The doctor comes, and tells me I am 1.5 cm dilated.

I do not understand. How is that possible? What's wrong? Why is my baby not here yet? And why does it start to hurt? I'm getting furious. Why would anyone in their right mind claim that there is such a thing as painless childbirth? Storytellers! Phonies! Birth hurts!!! The pain is agonizing and does not stop. I do not know when a contraction is beginning or ending. My belly is gripped in an unrelenting wrench. My husband and doula try to help me the best they can, but all I can is scream and rage, and beg for an epidural. When I finally get it, I feel instant relief. Exhausted and humbled by the nightmare I have just endured, I fall into a heavy sleep, grateful for a few quiet hours of rest. Now here is a pain-free labor. But that's not what I had in mind twenty four hours ago.

With the epidural, I dilate fully within two hours. My body has a chance to do what it had wanted to do all along: open up and give safe passage to my baby. All it took was two hours. The hours prior, it seemed, were a cruel joke. All that crazy pain, for this? I am deeply confused.

Confused, I start pushing. I push with my feet in stirrups, push squatting, push on my knees. But none of it makes sense. Not only do I not feel much from the waist down, even as the epidural is wearing of, but I have lost my agenda. If I'm not the one giving birth, who is?

Three hours later I haven't made much progress. Exhausted, I am facing another moment of truth: I can't go any longer. I had thought I could at least push my baby out, but the truth is, I can not. My doctor gives me two options: a C-section or vacuum extraction. I choose the latter.

When it is over and I hold my son in my arms, my confusion turns to wondrous awe. How can it be that this precious baby has come from me? How is this possible?

Each shaking, bliss-filled minute in the hours after birth is filled with speechless incomprehension of what had just happened. I can't believe that I've done it, but here it is: I have given birth. I did it. Or did I? Though proud of having survived the trial of birth, I do not feel the credit of this birth is mine, and I wanted to take credit for something. But what had I really done anyway? Wail and scream in fear. Give up. I know I had done the best I could, but I didn't think being able to hold my beautiful baby was my merit.

Some hours after birth I shuffle into the bathroom. I sit down on the toilet, feeling oddly empty. My baby is only a few feet away from me in the other room with my husband, but I feel far away and utterly alone. Surrounding me is only my breath, the beating of my heart, and the quiet humming of my postpartum body. I look down: my thighs are streaked with dried blood, my belly now soft and squishy like the cap of an oversized mushroom, my breasts heavy and full, gearing up for the promise of nursing. Looking at my body, I am humbled. You did this, I realize, you gave birth. You, my body.

My body had known how to birth my baby. It had known how to open, despite my fearsome meddling. This was the naked truth. It was also true that the epidural had been a blessing. But while it gave me relief, it didn't bail me out of my responsibility to see the truth about the pain I had endured in the hours of labor. The epidural didn't dispatch my birthing pains; it only postponed them. Weeks and months after my son was born, Birth and I had unfinished business left: the business of radical opening.

BIRTH IS WISE: HANNA'S BIRTH

Early motherhood was hard. Frustrated about lack of sleep, irritated by my baby's growing needs and will, resentful about the constant clutter in my house, and taxed with another pregnancy fourteen months later, I got frequently sick. And we are not talking the occasional seasonal cold here. I was sick. All. The. Time. When the day was done, with its running around and holding it together, I collapsed into bed at night. Like a weary warrior coming home from battle I skeptically rehearsed my "victories": I had successfully fought the toys on the floor, the clutter in the corners, a rambunctious boy who wouldn't nap, and, most of all, a reality of motherhood nothing and no one had prepared me for. I had merely survived another dozen waking hours.

In the fourth or fifth month of my second pregnancy, my body shut off its milk supply, force-weaning my 18 month old off his favorite food (though he did reclaim his place at breast when his sister was born). My husband was glad to see my body making a curtain call. Our active boy, my husband reasoned, did not need to sap my energy more than he did already. I did not argue with him, but I knew better. The problem was not my son and his wild energy, but my lack of care for myself and my amazing, hard-working body. I need my body, and my body needs me. This raw truth, however, I realized only when crisis forced me to listen.

Birth held me close during that time, urging me to admit to the truth of my pains, and to the truth of where I stood as a mother – not of where I wanted to be. My body kept record. It ached, shivered, groaned and burned, trying to help me settle my account with Birth. Listen, please listen, it said, you are being too hard on all of us. Let us enjoy each other. Breathe. Open. Let go. So I tried. I made efforts to listen to my body, and surrendered.

When I am in labor with my second baby, I am in bed. It is the middle of the night, and my husband and son are asleep in the other room. I'd been having regular contractions after tucking Felix into bed, contractions I'd been trying to ignore and mollify with a warm bath, to no avail. I had a long and tiring day with my toddler, and am bone tired. All I want is rest and sleep. I am hoping Birth can wait, at least one more day. But here she is: granting me another visit. She doesn't care about my wishes for delay. The time to answer her call is Now.

So I do. But instead of getting up like last time and rolling out the red carpet, I stay in bed. Excuse my casual welcome. Make yourself at home. Birth doesn't mind. She's been around and gets down to business. Hour after hour, the contractions roll in and out, steady and insistent like unanswered questions. I try to answer them, one at a time. I let go of memories and wishful thinking, and go inside. I feel my belly tightening, pulling, pressing ... pulling more... and more... and MORE and MORE!!! and releasing ... releasing ... resting. I am resting. It is quiet. The night is my womb. My son is sleeping. My daughter is on her way to be born. I hear my breath, and an early morning bird. Birth is nodding off for a spell, or so it seems. Then she stirs again, growing big in two or three breaths until she fills the whole universe. My belly is stretched across, sparkling and teeming with memories of everything that ever was, and ever will be. Birth inhales once more, illuminating each memory to the threshold of recognition – when she withdraws and settles again into the sheets of my bed.

So we breathe and dance. Hours and lifetimes pass, though I have no concept of it. Dancing with Birth, I have no concepts for anything, not for time, self, or pain. All I know is that my body is Now resting... Now tightening... Now howling with the memories of stars – but I can't call it pain. I am not calling it anything at all. I let it call me: Open, it says. Oooooooooopen! Sometimes this call roars like a thousand water falls, sometimes it's barely a whisper. But it's always there, reverberating in the liquid traffic of my cells as they move with the speed of light between worlds. All I do is listen. Listen to the swell of contractions as they roll in on the sleeves of Birth. Bow my head and take a breath as Birth swoops me up and sends me across the Milky Way.

It is still dark when I get up. I do not know what drives me out of bed. The house is quiet, and I have no thoughts or plans. Still, I know it is time. Time to meet my baby. I wake my husband who wakes my son. On my way to the bathroom, my water breaks. I double over and fold into myself on hands and knees. I move without volition, moaning like ancient mountain caves as Birth speeds up her steps. I try to keep up, breathing and listening to the new dance moves she is teaching me. Not much else matters.

The next thing I know is that I am in the backseat of our car, driving to the birth center ... that someone offers me a wheelchair in a brightly lit hallway which I refuse because sitting down now is madness ... that I am on a bed, half naked. My whole body trembles and shakes. Herds of wild horses are galloping through my pelvis. Meteors from faraway galaxies are crashing through my bones. There is nothing holding them back. I am the earth and the quake, the ocean and the tidal wave. A power unlike anything I've ever known reaches into me and calls my name. Or is it the name of my daughter? I can not tell. I only know there is nothing left of me. I gave Birth everything I had. There is one last sound that erupts from my mouth, one primal, earth splitting AAAAAAAAlmighty howl – and my baby flushes forth from my body.

Within minutes, the waves recede. Birth is gathering her cape and nods to say good-bye. I can feel the glow of her smile on my skin.

This, and nothing less, is what Birth wants from you: to go along with her wherever she takes you. To take a full-body, head-first plunge into this breath and the next, saying Yes! and Yes! again to the wild adventure of each moment. It is the adventure of your lifetime, the resounding echo of an agreement you made decades and eons ago when you first said Yes to this lifetime, to being on earth, to being born. Birth wants nothing new from you. She won't ask you anything you don't already know. Give her your wholehearted Yes, and she will dance with you in wisely measured ways. She will give you space to grow and time to rest, peak after valley after peak after valley. Birth's wisdom is in her pacing. Everything has its place. Follow her cadence. There is no other place to go. Be the storm, and sweep across the sky. Be the stillness in the quiet folds of labor, sweet heaviness of flesh and bones.

BIRTH IS WILD: SASKIA'S BIRTH

After Hanna's birth I thought I knew everything there was to know about Birth. I had heard about the old wives' tale that third babies are a wildcard when it comes to their birth, but I wasn't troubled. Wildcard or not, I had danced with Birth before and was certain I would remember how to be with her when she called again. And indeed, I did remember. Until it was time for a new lesson.

Birth arrives again late in the day. I am in bed, and stay there throughout the night. Labor is sweet and simple, proceeding like rainfall or the burning of stars – a still life robed in the cloak of night. My body is opening. I am having my baby. The sensations of labor are strong and powerful, but they are not painful. They howl and roar and pass through me like gusts of wind over open prairie, finding nothing to catch or overthrow.

When dawn breaks, I get out of bed. My body remembers. It is time, again. Soon after, my water breaks, cracking my body open like a shell. This isn't the illusive surfing of dilation anymore, but the eager crashing to shore. Having planned a home birth this time, I step into the birthing tub, ready to receive my baby. I push two or three times, but nothing happens. This is unlike her older sister who slid from my body with only a couple of contractions. Up until this point everything had gone very much like Hanna's labor. Birth and I had been humming along, but now things feel different. I push for twenty minutes, for an hour. Still, no baby. Instead, labor starts to hurt. Doubt nags behind my temples. What is going on? Why is my baby not coming? Fear readily joins the party. What if the baby is stuck? What if I can't push her out? My moaning pitches to screaming; my body grips and tightens. I stare into the water like into a crystal ball, fixating on dancing flecks of light as if they could reveal to me what is wrong.

Nothing happens. Minutes pass. I am lost. This I hadn't expected: that Birth would change on me, switch direction, shrug off our dance agreement with rash abandon. I feel small and vulnerable, a lonely soul in the middle of nowhere. No matter how well I danced with Birth before, it is all now just a memory. I am at a loss of what to do. Nothing that worked before is working now; no breathing, no centering, no touch, nor words of support. How to go on from here?

Suddenly, it is obvious. There is only one place to go, and it is screaming at the top of my lungs. How could I not hear it? I had to go toward the pain. Leave behind the fantasy of Birth I had created, and open up to a whole new side of her. Her wild side.

Birth is not civil. She follows her own laws. She is messy, noisy and adventurous, churning the wheels of creation with her wildness. In this, she reminds me of how my children painted when they were younger. They loaded their brushes generously with yellows, reds and blues, not concerned with drips on the floor or streaks of color running down their painting while whipping curious shapes and splotches on the easel of their imagination. They improvised, adjusted, re-invented, and were always proud of their creation.

So is Birth, unconcerned about what I am thinking, assured of her wild power. But Birth is patient, even in her wildness. Sitting in the birthing tub, moaning in pain, she didn't rush me to make my move. Instead, Birth keeps reminding me that it is my turn to follow suit, contraction after gripping contraction. Be wild, she implored, forget yourself! Don't hold back!

But am I? I want this baby with all my heart, my womb is open, and my midwives, family and friends are endorsing my commitment with quiet cheer. However, as time passes I find myself more and more distracted, self-conscious, and in pain. Where is this coming from? What is this pain about? With each contraction my body freezes, focusing my mind on the single task of figuring out an answer. I am drawn into my head where I observe a quagmire of choking, sloshing thoughts, nipping and competing to be lifted into the light of consciousness. I stare at the churning mess, growing desperate, when out of it rises a virgin thought, throbbing and stubborn. It is not a pretty thought, but pretty or not, it clings to recognition for dear life. It lobbies and urges, fishing for syllables and syntax, until it find its way into my throat and onto my tongue.

"I don't want to poop into the water!", I yell. There. It is out. For a moment, the words bounce on the surface of the warm water, pristine receiving blanket for my sweet baby, and are promptly caught by my midwives. "Oh, don't you worry about this, dear", they chime, "we have a little fishing net we can use to get things out."

I don't know if it was hearing my midwives' support, or me speaking my fear, but I feel instant relief. The pain subsides, and I feel my baby move. The next few contractions are majestic; Birth had successfully pulled me over to her wild side, and I am catching up with her. I don't care if I soil the water or what anyone is thinking, but let down my guard and push as if there is no tomorrow. The next thing I know, my baby is crowning: exposing soft ridges of skin over bone beneath a weaving shock of silky hair. I reach down to touch her crown, and my fingers meet the softest, sweetest, most sublime arrangement of matter imaginable.

A couple of contractions later, my daughter Saskia is born. I lift her up to my chest, waiting for her to arrive in her naked body and open her eyes. A few moments pass, but her body remains heavy and limp. My heart flutters in panic. Is she okay? My midwives start rubbing her down with dry towels. They work with purpose and measured haste. "Breathe for your baby", they tell me reassuringly, and that's what I do. Birth was not yet done, still holding me accountable and dancing her wild dance. I bow my head and agree to do my part. Breathe. Breathe slowly. Breathe deeply. Just breathe.

When Saskia wakes up, her eyes rest quietly on the faces around her. She does not cry, not that day, and not for many days. My husband and older two children hug, hold and kiss her, and after the cord is cut and the placenta born, I start nursing her while my midwives give me strengthening herbs to drink and clean up the birthing tub.

I don't know if they had to pull out their fishing net. Maybe they did, maybe they didn't. It didn't matter. What mattered is that I let go, let go of it all: fear, inhibitions, expectations, ego, blood, sweat, and then some more. It was then, and only then, that Birth was satisfied. If she is asking you to go wild, meet her with a roar. She doesn't take No for an answer.

BIRTH IS PATIENT

Labor is the main stage of Birth but not her only domain. Often labor doesn't go as planned, and sometimes it doesn't happen at all (such as with emergency or scheduled C-sections). But Birth is not dismayed. She will claim her time, often after the baby is born.

The prime role of Birth is to bring things into being so that they may live. This requires radical opening and parting with what doesn't serve the new any longer. For a fruit to become a fruit, it needs to leave the state of bud and shed the blossoms that have surrounded it. For a woman to become mother, she needs to let go of wishful thinking, clinging and other childish ways. This usually doesn't happen overnight (or however long labor lasts). It is a gradual process, a mounting of capacity, a ripening. At what moment in time can we say that a mountain stream is born a river?

Birth persists. She will not leave until what needs to be born is born, and the new is secured. To expect that she has accomplished her work upon first delivery is to miss her scope. Birth will standby to ensure that her charges *thrive*.

After my babies were born, I still had a lot to learn about being a mother. This was often as painful as going through labor. In the years that followed, Birth was quite busy reminding me to continue what I'd started in the wake of contractions: to breathe, to open, to be vulnerable and accept what is. To be expansive and big. To be truthful, and yes, sometimes wild. To acknowledge when I am in pain, and listen to my body.

Over time, Birth has less frequently knocked on my door, reassured that her children, and I, as a mother, are thriving. There are still times when she grants me a visit, now that my babies are well on their way to becoming adults. I am glad Birth has been patient with me. Reminding me to be patient has been one of her most important teachings, suspended in the slow-effacing memory of letting go.

BIRTH IS BEAUTIFUL

Patience opens our eyes to beauty: the beauty of the rise and fall of a sleeping baby's chest, a sobbing kiss, of uninhibited playful anarchy. Looking back to the years of mothering and my children's births, what stands out, golden haloed, are the unhurried, patient moments. When I was able to silence the harrowing beat of shoulds and schedules, egos and wills, beauty blossomed. I remembered that something precious was happening *here, right now*. I remembered to fall in love.

Birth awakens this memory. She beckons us to forget our busy occupations and remember what it's like to be alive and real. Definite and instantaneous, she draws our attention with the power of thunder. Look, she urges, look right here. Listen, smell, feel and taste *everything*. I made it all for you. Be my lover, and let me be yours. Be here with me and stay.

When I was in high school, we studied Goethe's "Faust". In this old German story, Doctor Faust, a highly successful but restless and dissatisfied scholar, sets out to find the true essence of life ("was die Welt im Innersten zusammenhält"). In his eagerness, he makes a deal with Mephistopheles, a force of darkness and cunning. Faust promises Mephistopheles his soul should he ever find happiness. After many years of striving, this moment indeed arrives. For the first time, Faust experiences happiness. Content with whatever is or will be, he cries out "Verbleibe doch! Du bist so schön!" ("Stay! Thou art so beautiful!"). Mephistopheles promptly arrives to take Faust's soul, hoping to cheat the forces of Light out of what belongs to them. But his effort is in vain. Faust gets carried away by heavenly angels, and Mephistopheles loses the bargain. Faust, who spent all his life striving, never at peace, was redeemed when he found beauty. At the moment of surrender, he was free.

Birth wants nothing less for you. She wants you to stop and be real. Get close and dissolve in the rapture of each blessed moment. Give her your humble, naked self, your tender wondrous veneration, and Birth will set you free.

Birth Time

There is time, and there is
Birth Time.
One is born of the world
of schedules, alarm clocks, meal times.
The other of the world of transitions
Where souls are fitting for bodies costumed
For life.
Measured only
By the beat of the universe
Not by the clock's iron hands
Birth Time is
Night and Day woven
Into the humming fabric of skin folding into itself.
Is awareness of body
Seams splitting and joining in try-outs for a
Masterpiece.
Is being the needle
And the needle's eye
threading your prayers.

-Author

GOING THROUGH IT

I didn't want to send this book out into the world without a few words about the physiological process of labor. To help you deepen your understanding of labor and birth and your role in it, I have added questions for self-inquiry and practice suggestions. Feel free to keep a journal as you reflect on the questions, or pause at times and meditate on the reading. If you want to supplement the information in this chapter, please refer to the list of common labor terms in the appendix and to other information resources.

Labor has three major phases. The first phase accomplishes full dilation (widening) and effacement (thinning) of the mother's cervix. The second phase is the pushing or birthing phase and ends with the delivery of the baby. During the final phase the placenta is birthed.

First Phase: Dilation and Effacement

The first phase of labor can be divided into four parts:

1. Pre-labor
2. Early labor
3. Active labor
4. Transition

PRE-LABOR marks the beginning of the first phase of labor. During this phase, your body is gearing up for birth: blood volume increases, Braxton-Hicks contractions (which are painless) become more frequent, your mammary glands start to produce colostrum (baby's first food), your cervix begins to soften, and you may lose your mucus plug (a blood-tinged, snotty looking glob that seals the cervix). These signs can occur days and weeks before your first actual labor contraction, go often unnoticed, and don't necessarily predict when your uterus will kick into gear. This can be frustrating, especially if the due date comes and goes.

Many mothers who get to that point try to get labor going – as I did when I was past my due date with my son. There are many ways to naturally induce labor but I believe an effective natural induction method is to be stress free and calm. Your body opens more easily when it feels safe. It helps to be in the right "mood". I wonder to this day whether my son would have been born closer to his due date if I had been less anxious. Because when I had stopped fretting and was at peace with myself and the world, labor began.

Meditating on the softening of your cervix is a wonderful way to connect with your body and baby towards the end of pregnancy. You are not quite in labor and not feeling much, but your body is already working on the Grand Opening. As your cervix is softening, so you too may become more thin-skinned. You may feel irritable, weepy, vulnerable. You feel the world inside and outside more intensely. Little things matter. Everything may get through to you more quickly as your cervix is beginning to melt. Feelings can run high. Now is a good time to go inside of yourself. Do you have thoughts or feelings that feel thick, dense, stubborn, un-yielding? Are there situations or people you approach with a closed-off attitude? Do as your cervix: soften grudges and thin out your fears. The power of your cervix rests in its disappearance: Only when she is gone can your baby be born.

Reflection

How do you feel about your due date? How important is it for you? How does your partner feel about it? Are you in agreement?

How do you imagine passing time during pre-labor? Will it be a time of waiting, keeping busy, worrying? What do you typically do when you wait?

Practice

Throughout your day, notice when you are waiting for something (for a green traffic light, for your iPhone to load etc). Notice what waiting feels like in your body. What thoughts come up? How are you breathing? What is the underlying feeling of waiting? Boredom, tiredness, fear, something else?

Acknowledge whatever feelings come up. Place both hands on your belly and take a deep, slow breath. Keeping your gaze soft, let your eyes slowly move around your field of vision. Let them rest at random on far places and closeup. As you let your eyes wander, continue to notice your hands on your belly. What do you see?

EARLY LABOR is a time of transition. The first labor signs are your body's invitation to start paying attention and may include menstrual-like cramps in your lower belly and/or back, mild diarrhea, and the rupture of the amniotic bag. They are a gentle beckoning to heed the rhythm of Birth as it begins to flow through your body. Early labor is the resounding echo of births past, calling you to follow its bidding. You do so by turning your listening inward. That doesn't mean you have to stop what you are doing or move into a labor position. It may actually be better to carry on with whatever you are doing as this can keep your mind from wandering and provides a comforting backdrop for the new rhythm beginning to take hold within you. In early labor, the rhythm of Birth is honored by becoming more mindful, by looking beneath the appearance of daily routines and connecting to the secret pulse of the body. In doing so, you enter into dialog with yourself, your body, and the command of Birth.

Reflection

How aware are you of transitions that occur throughout your day? Do you notice when they are happening?

Which transitions are easy for you, and which ones are harder?

Think of a frequently occurring transition from a fairly comfortable experience to a more uncomfortable one. What is your usual response?

Practice

Notice when you are about to transition from one activity to another (e.g. getting ready to stand up from sitting, leaving home to go to work etc). Take a moment to pause. Close your eyes if you can safely do so. Bring your attention to the sounds around you. Notice sounds arising and fading, near and far. As they come and go, notice patterns. What do you hear?

ACTIVE LABOR is the time in labor when things are getting done. Your uterus, endocrine and limbic system have established their conference call and are talking business. With contractions coming more regularly and consistently, about every two to five minutes, your body is urging you to submerse yourself in the work of labor and become fully committed. At this point you may start seeking positions that increase your comfort, make contractions more efficient, and allow you to go further within. However, not all mothers have the desire to change positions frequently. I found it quite hard to move around and be "active" when I was in labor. It was easier to stay (and rest) in the same position, and focus on the *movement inside*. Position changes were prompted instinctively by sensations of discomfort (both physically and emotionally), and by changes in the labor flow.

Reflection

What does "active" mean to you? Do you consider yourself an active person? What does it look like when you are actively engaged with a project, task or idea? What does your partner notice about you?

How might being "active" in birth differ from other times?

What helps you maintain focus? What environment works best for you? Do you like it quiet, or have music/TV on? Are you easily distracted by other people?

Practice

Choose one auditory, one visual and one kinesthetic meditation object from the list below, and focus on each for two to three minutes. Notice which object supports your focus best.

Auditory: naturally occurring sounds, a music recording, a voice recording, the sound of your breath

Visual: a picture or photograph, a flower, a candle, a mental image

Tactile: the movement of your breath (diaphragm, ribcage), your pulse, your skin against clothes

TRANSITION is marked by the final opening of the cervix. Mothers often become more restless, feel hot or cold, shiver and shake, feel nauseous, and find it generally difficult to get comfortable. They start to seek (and may insist on) places and positions that maximize their effort to deliver the baby. Earlier preferences about where and how to birth the baby are often abandoned (including birth tubs and squatting positions). Contractions may feel like they are back to back; the body appears to completely take over. At this point in labor, mothers often feel overwhelmed and out of control. They may become more vocal (moan, groan, cry out) and say that they can't do it anymore.

Reflection

What is your primary response when you are at your edge (e.g. hold a yoga pose, are hungry, tired, in conflict, fearful or anxious)? What feeling(s) come up spontaneously when you *can't do this anymore*?

What do you tend to do in response to these feelings (what is your secondary response)? Do you move closer to the edge (fight), run away (flight), or do something else?

Practice

> Notice when you are reaching the edge of your comfort zone. Make sure you feel safe before moving on with this practice.
>
> Pay attention to your primary response. Typical reactions can include aversion, resistance, vulnerability, rebellion, curiosity.
>
> Notice what you may want to do about your initial feeling (run, push through, go numb, withdraw etc)? This is your secondary response. Notice this too, but don't act on it. Stay put without trying to change anything. Instead, surrender. Accept that what you are experiencing may be difficult, uncomfortable, or painful. Accept that you may not know how you will come through this. Remind yourself that you will.

Second Phase: Baby's Birth

The second phase of labor begins when your cervix is fully dilated and your uterus gears up to push your baby out. Initially, contractions may be more spread out as the uterus communicates the next set of instructions with its "team members" (hormones, neurotransmitters, nerves). This is a great time to catch your breath. You are on the threshold of greeting your baby. You may or may not feel a spontaneous urge to push, and as long as your baby doesn't need to be born quickly due to a medical emergency, keep breathing and wait. Traditionally called the "pushing stage", many mothers and their partners are relieved when they reach full dilation, and they want to do just that: push. After the full surrender of dilation, there is finally something to do! It may be difficult to resist the urge to move things along and wait for the body's urge to push. But pregnancy, labor and birth are very much about waiting. They are an invitation to traverse the slow-meandering margins of transformation with unhurried faith.

Try to resist the temptation to push, and let your baby *labor down*. Laboring down lets your uterus continue to do the work, as it should be. As long as you are contracting, your uterus will continue to move your baby down into the birth canal. As your baby has moved lower, pressure will build in your rectum and pelvic floor, and the urge to push will increase. At this point you may instinctively start to bear down. Just as in other phases of labor, this can take minutes or hours but eventually your baby will start to crown. This is accompanied by a burning sensation around the circumference of your vagina, called the "Ring of Fire". Though this sensation is short-lived and paralleled with other strong sensations, it helps to continue to breathe and to relax your jaw and pelvic floor.

Reflection

Do you ever get impatient? How do you know when you are? What does impatience feel like to you: anxious, irritable, annoyed, restless, eager, overwhelmed?

Notice if you feel an urge to act on your impatience. Next shift your focus to your breathing. According to brain scientist Jill Bolte Taylor,[2] spontaneous emotions such as impatience have a ninety second shelf-life in our brains. Chemicals produced in response to a triggering situation are metabolized within this amount of time – unless we engage in thoughts and behaviors that re-stimulate the chemical processes that caused the reaction in the first place. Give yourself ninety seconds to wait, breathe and see what happens. Instead of reacting, accept your breath as a viable mode of transportation.

Practice: Elimination Meditation

A great way to prepare for the second phase of labor is to practice patience while having a bowel movement. When you near your baby's birth during labor, you may feel intense pressure in your lower pelvis and rectum. These sensations are very similar to the need for a bowel movement. Effective pushing in childbirth is aimed at the rectum. It utilizes a skill you have familiarized yourself with thousands of times when relieving yourself on the toilet. Next time you need to go (and especially when you are constipated), try this meditation.

1. Notice the buildup of fullness in your bowels.
2. Wait until this fullness demands that you go to the toilet.
3. Sit on the toilet.
4. Wait. Don't push or do anything. Keep your jaw relaxed. Breathe normally. Rest.
5. Notice the sensations in your rectum and anal sphincter.
6. Notice the sensations of peristalsis in your large intestines (wave-like muscle contractions that move food down the digestive tract).
7. Observe your reactions to these sensations, in particular feelings of impatience (e.g. frustration, apprehension, discomfort, embarrassment, concern).
8. Notice the impulse to hold your breath and push. Does this impulse come from willful desire? Are you trying to get it over with? Push through discomfort or pain? Control possible fears? Or does it come as

---

2   Jill Bolte Taylor, *My Stroke of Insight* (Penguin Group, 2006).

a spontaneous nudge from your body to move things along? Who is doing the pushing?

9. Experiment with changing your position. Try squatting or leaning your torso in different directions.

10. Experiment with making sound. Try exhaling with a sigh.

11. Repeat steps 4 through 10 until finished.

Third Phase: Birth of the Placenta

The last phase of labor is marked by the delivery of the placenta and the cutting of the umbilical cord. After your baby is born, your uterus will continue to contract to separate the placenta from the uterine wall and expel it. This can take up to thirty minutes. These contractions are usually milder than the contractions before your baby's birth. Plus, you are hopefully holding your baby! Your midwives and doctor will keep an eye on this aspect of labor to make sure your placenta is safely delivered. If needed, they may massage your belly and/or give you a dose of Pitocin to assist your body's effort to release the placenta. The umbilical cord can be cut before or after this has happened. If you decide to cut the umbilical cord before the placenta is born, you may want to wait until the cord stops pulsating. This has many health benefits for your baby.

Reflection

The delivery of the placenta finalizes the physical separation of mother and child. It is the end of childbirth and the end of a nine month dream time filled with fantasies and anticipation. What are your dreams about your baby, about birth, and about yourself as a mother?

Practice

Before you go to sleep tonight, spend a few minutes in quiet meditation. Bring your awareness to the space between the eye brows, also called the third eye. In yoga, this area is connected to our ability to envision and see clearly. Keep your forehead relaxed and your eyes soft as you focus on this area. Continue to breathe quietly. Try to refrain from fantasizing about your baby's birth or thinking about your birth plan. Instead, welcome Birth into your awareness. Ask her kindly to show you what you need; ask for a dream. After this, retire to sleep.

Tomorrow morning, upon first waking (or when waking in the middle of the night), become aware of your body and any lingering dreams. Notice your overall feeling and mood. They may point you to an exchange that may have occurred between you and Birth that night.

ODE TO BREATH

One of the main strategies pregnant women often think of when they imagine themselves in labor utilizes the breath. Thanks to French obstetrician Dr. Fernand Lamaze who, back in the 1940s, popularized breathing techniques during childbirth, the collective consciousness of mothers-to-be now counts the breath as a powerful tool in labor. And it is indeed.

Free, portable and readily accessible, our breath is the only body function that is both voluntary and involuntary, i.e. we can use it intentionally to lower stress and pain. Conscious, deep breathing lowers cortisol levels and slows down physiological processes that interfere with effective cellular functioning, calms the nervous system, improves blood circulation, recharges energy and relieves fatigue and pain caused by compression of nerve endings, and increases oxygen supply to the uterus and brain. Greater mental clarity, muscle and organ functioning ensue. But breathing has not only physiological benefits. It is a direct gateway to the present moment.

To benefit from the breath in this manner, we first need to become aware that we breathe. This is usually the hardest part. The mind, restless by nature, is easily bored with something so basic and repetitive as the breath. But when we do take interest in the process of breathing, magic can happen. We start to sense that we are beholding something rare and precious. Intrigued, we pursue. We follow our breath like steps into an enchanted, long forgotten land. It is the land of timeless transformation, of never ending renewal and change.

To remember our breath is to remember, in our very body, that change is constant. The breath always moves. Inhale gives way to exhale and exhale to inhale. Nothing stays the same. Not our breath, not our body, not our thoughts, not our experience or sense of self. We may not be always aware of this message, but our breath recounts this story with each inhale and exhale: All is change. Labor contractions, no matter how intense they get, won't last forever. They are transient like the breath.

To utilize the magic of breathing in labor, simply welcome your breath. My first yoga teacher always opened her classes with the words, "Welcome your breath." When I began teaching myself, I adopted this invitation for my own classes. I would offer it as the opening phrase for a centering meditation, as a standalone during asana practice, or as a "wake up call" to signal the end of final relaxation. Over the years, this simple mantra has forged a decent track in my brain and helps me shift into more mindful gears when I am on emotional autopilot. I remember to welcome my breath. Quite often, this welcoming is not more than a modest acknowledgment of my breathing. It doesn't change my breath or stop me in my tracks. And yet, it is a profound welcoming. Like the arrival of rain after a hot, long summer, it brings relief. Our breath is life, literally. This is where it all starts: our existence on this planet, our intent to be nowhere else but here, our resolve to welcome whatever Birth asks of us when we are in labor. Birth may ask many things of you when the time comes, but foremost it will be this: to remember to breathe. Always. Your breath moves the gears of change.

Welcoming your breath is to acknowledge this change as a process of alchemical proportions. When you take a breath in awareness, it takes you right into the middle of the present moment. Like an arrow shot into the air, you may not know where you will land, but you will land somewhere real. If you like, do a little experiment right now and see where you land. Put the book down, and notice your breath.

What did you notice? Where did you land? What did the present feel like? Maybe it felt calm, maybe it contained an itch or irritation. Your experience of the present is not always pleasant, at least initially. You may notice boredom, numbness, indifference, excitement, discomfort, and in labor, fear or pain. Tuning into your breath will land you somewhere on this spectrum. There you are. You may not like where you land, but it's always a bull's eye. You are exactly where you need to be: at the place of transformation.

Move with the tide of your breath. Soar with the inhale and sigh with the exhale. Go with your laboring body's rhythm and its ups and downs. Don't worry about how to breathe. Just make sure you do. In fact, don't worry about anything. Go beneath the temporal and transient. Touch the hem of God, or whatever holy name suits you.

CALLING BABY HOME

Sound rides on the waves of the breath and is a powerful tool in labor. Harnessing sound through vocalizing (toning, moaning, chanting, humming) is as old as the world. It is a mother's roaring agreement to follow Birth's bidding and call her baby home. Many women use sound while laboring, and this makes perfect sense: it doesn't require any setup or team effort and, like our breath, is instantly available. When we make sound, we extend beyond the limits of our physical body. We gain larger footprint.

Vocalizing in labor has also physiological benefits. It unhinges the jaw and relaxes the cervix, vagina and pelvic floor. The mechanism responsible for this effect is a neural pathway that initiates an involuntary reflex action, the so-called reflex arc. Reflex arcs bypass conscious thought and cause a spontaneous response to a stimulus. A well-known example is the knee jerk reflex.

To observe the reflex arc between your jaw and pelvic floor, you can try this simple exercise. (You may want to read this paragraph first as it is helpful to close your eyes for this exercise). Start by taking a deep breath. Exhale with your mouth open, and release your jaw. Now notice your pelvic floor. Get a sense of its tone and tension. Take one or two more slow breaths. Then, while keeping your attention on your pelvic floor, slowly close your mouth, tighten your jaw and clench your teeth. Notice what happens to the muscles in your vagina, cervix and pelvic floor, and what happens to your breathing. Take another breath and release your jaw with your exhale. Again, pay attention to changes in your pelvic floor.

The changes with this exercise are often quite subtle, and you may or may not have noticed a difference. When we tense the jaw, the muscles in the lower pelvis contract as well, and when we loosen the jaw, the pelvic floor softens. Low pitch vocalizing on exhalation reinforces the relaxation response. "Aaaaaahh" and "Ooooooohh" sounds are particularly effective in labor. They are vibrationally connected to the sacred sound of the universe: Aum. The sound of Aum captures the whole of creation and, according to yoga scriptures, God's creative plan: A represents *akara*, creative vibration, U is *ukara*, the force which preserves and sustains, and M is *makara*, the vibratory power of disintegration and dissolution.

Birth is all three: creation, preservation, and dissolution. A child is born, a new human life begins. The cosmic cycle of birth and rebirth repeats. The Buddha said it's extremely rare and fortunate to be born a human. To explain the auspiciousness of human birth, he told the following story: Imagine the earth totally covered with water. A yoke with a single hole is floating on the waves. Strong winds push the yoke this way and that way, at random intervals. Every one hundred years a blind sea turtle comes up from beneath the waves and happens to stick its head through the yoke. That's how rare it is to be born a human.

How incomprehensible and fortunate indeed that you will be giving birth to a child! Each labor contraction is cause for celebration and thanksgiving. Give praise at the top of your lungs, or within the silent folds of your heart. Not all women make sound in labor. Some are very quiet, like one of my yoga students whose birth I attended. When I arrived at her home, she was resting on a couch with her eyes closed. I could only tell by her breathing when she was having a contraction. Her breath moved like the curtains in her open windows, billowing and dancing with the hot summer breeze. Time passed, the sun moved, flowers opened and closed, plums ripened. There was never a more beautiful song, and no doubt that she was calling her baby home. Her quiet focus was almost audible, and erupted, unmistakably, from the lungs of her son when he emerged from her womb.

NUMBERS

As I am coming to the end of this chapter and my reflections on how to know Birth, I have one more suggestion: Forget the numbers.

Going through birth is a deeply reflective experience. Not only does it reflect who you are and what you are capable of but it also reflects the matrix of Life. This matrix is made up of single moments of countless shapes and forms. In birth, they can only be known through the crucible of surrender. They can't be counted, measured or cataloged. Still, we try. Living in a number-loving culture, we have given Birth her share of statistics and appraisal. We set a due date, measure dilation and effacement, assess pain levels, time contractions.

Numbers can be important to confirm progress or to necessitate intervention, but it is easy to fall under their spell. We like to believe in numbers. Two and two is always four. One is never zero. But Birth does not care about numbers. She does not come with a wrist watch. Her step is not measured in inches. Birth exists in this moment only, breathing and rocking Earth's children to shore. Get into the boat with her, and let the stars be your navigation.

This takes faith, faith I did not have when I was in labor for the first time. I timed my contractions, followed the 4-1-1 rule, and had my cervix checked soon after I got to the hospital. I watched the clock. Numbers ruled. But instead of giving me reassurance, they made me only more anxious.

In our last Yoga Way to Birth class, couples practice a labor rehearsal using yoga postures for simulated contractions. Mothers have a chance to put into practice what they have learned in class while being supported by their partners. At some point during the rehearsal, I ask if couples want to know how far they have "dilated". Some go for it, others decline. I have noticed that the mothers who are on the more anxious side are more likely to want to find out. Doubtful about their progress, they seek an external reference point. However, this is never an objective one. While numbers may look neutral on a piece of paper, they often mean a great deal to us. We either feel good about them or we don't. During the labor rehearsal, I intentionally choose a lower number when I announce "dilation". Inevitably, mothers are dismayed. I certainly was when I heard that I was "only" one and a half centimeter after seven hours of active labor. For me, things went downhill from there.

During the rehearsal I encourage couples to become aware of their reaction, and to return to their mindfulness practice. I remind them to take a breath and avoid placing a value judgment on the information they've just received. I tell them to stay present and with what can be known in this moment only. Everything else is fiction.

Consider the following scenario: You decide to have your cervix checked after being in active labor for eight hours, and your doctor or midwife tells you that you are five centimeters dilated. A few hours pass, and you ask to be checked again. You are at six. Does this mean that labor has slowed down? If we correlate dilation with the hours that have passed, that appears to be the case. But can we say this with confidence?

Not necessarily. What we do know is that a certain numerical value was measured at a certain point in time. You may be a day away from meeting your baby, or Birth may surprise you with a sprint to the finish line. As a doula, I have seen mothers dilate several centimeter in less than an hour. You may wonder if there is anything you can do to affect Birth's timing. How about labor positions? Breathing techniques? Massage? Visualizations? The couples in my classes are always eager to learn them, and we have fun practicing the various positions and techniques. I remind them that these techniques can help ease the pain of the laboring body but they may not change the beat of Birth's drumming. At best, they can help you dance. When have you danced the last time just for the sake of dancing? Can you dance without looking at the clock? Forget the numbers. Count each blessed moment instead.

Love

To serve and never be tired is love.
To learn and never be filled is devotion.
To offer and never to end is surrender.

~Sri Chinmoy

With the body as our guide, we begin to feel, perhaps for the first time in our lives, that with our body, we are in the presence of a force and intelligence that is filled with wisdom, that is loving, flawlessly reliable, and strange to say, worthy of our deepest devotion.

~Reggie Ray

There are two things most pregnant women think about when anticipating labor and birth: to have a health baby, and get through it. The rest, a natural birth, manageable pain, laboring in a tub, is icing on the cake. What women rarely think about is to *love* being in labor. What is there to love anyhow? Labor hurts, it's unpredictable, and largely out of our control. Not an attractive bunch to fall in love with, eh? Besides, you also have to content yourself with your birth partners, medical staff, (family members?), and what you bring to labor in your mind and heart. How can you possibly love *all this*?

The love you may already have for your baby is a good start but it may be impractical to think that it's enough to guide you through labor. It's a romantic idea and super sweet and I wish this love all the power in the world, but expect that it will be tested and put under pressure. Lots of pressure. Contraction after contraction.

A love bigger than you've ever known is called for. A love all inclusive, unconditional, unwavering. A love that extends into the deepest recesses of your body and mind, dark, cowardly places and all, and into the farthest reaches of the cosmos. How to do this, I do not know. I won't be able to tell you how to be an angel. But I can tell you where to start, and this is right here, in your very body.

YOUR BEST FRIEND

When I taught prenatal yoga, we always did a check-in at the beginning of class. Women shared how far along they were, and how their body was feeling. Looking for camaraderie and counsel, they talked about being tired, short of breath, having back pain, heartburn, and not sleeping well. What stood out for me with those check-ins was that the women almost always talked about what was *not* working with their body, how their body hurt or failed to cooperate. I remember doing the same when I was pregnant myself: complaining to my husband about being nauseous, or begrudging the fact that I was tired. Rarely did I appreciate how hard my body was working, or bothered to ask why I was so uncomfortable with it. Was it even still my body? It didn't fit into my old clothes anymore, dragged its feet, couldn't stomach a big breakfast, huffed when climbing stairs, and passed out after each meal. The changes were literally breathtaking. Month after pregnant month, everything I had loved about my body was stripped away: my girlish frame, my quick step, my spryness and brawny vigor. The more my belly grew, the less I recognized myself, and a makeover was called for. It was high time to learn from my body.

When a woman gets pregnant, her body accepts the challenge instantly. It doesn't need a reminder or coaching to adjust to the new status quo. It quietly adapts, and doesn't mind the extra workload. After all, it gets to make a masterpiece! Can you follow your body's gracious example? Can you accept its invitation? Your body is your best friend, and this is what it wants you to do: be pregnant. Embrace your pregnant body, heaviness, slowness, aches and all. This is how you get ready for birth. Think of it: What we call pregnancy discomforts are invitations to be present. This also applies to symptoms that may require medical attention. They are your body's way to get your attention because your body needs you to be on board. It needs you to listen and to respect what you hear. This won't take all day. Modest and forgiving, the body doesn't ask for much – but it will ask. Give it some time, some care, and it will become tender in the wake of your tending.

Pregnancy is a time of tending. Not only is your body carrying out its usual functions but tending to the growth of your baby: building blood volume, digesting food and routing nutrients through the placenta, multiplying cells to make bones, organs, fingers and toes. Your body is working hard 24/7. Most of the time we take this for granted. I sure did. While I did make time to go to yoga now and then, or sit down with a cup of tea, I mostly ignored my body. I tried to carry on with business as usual. My cup of tea sat cooling on the counter. Always on the run, attempting to keep up with schedules, personal expectations and (after becoming a mother) the demands of my young children, I liked to pretend that my body didn't exist. Only when I went to yoga class did my body's quiet truth surface. It felt bone tired, achy, heavy and tense. It pleaded with me. Notice me. Help me out. Listen. Okay, I consented, I'll listen. But only for 10 minutes. When the bell chimes we'll get up and go. I have to be someplace. My weekly self-care rations were puny but my body refused to be ignored. It kept handing me high price tags for negligence: A week in bed with the flu. Months of irritability and crankiness. Frequent trips to the chiropractor to heal my weeping back. Thank you very much.

Our body truly cares for us. It tries to protect, comfort and support. Generally forgiving and generous, it allows us our independence and freedom and lets us get away with things. But the body is not negligent in its caring. It keeps up with our unhealthful habits for only so long and, when enough is enough, puts on the brakes to have a chat with us. By that time we are often already sick, injured, or mentally at risk. Body-bound, we are forced to do time – time tending to one of our most fundamental relationships: the relationship with our body.

This relationship, like any relationship we rely on and want to benefit from, is reciprocal by nature. We take, we give. Acknowledge your body regularly, not only when it is convenient or when you are in pain. Frequently, ask your body for what it needs, and try to act on its feedback. When hungry, find food. (Real food that is. A bag of chips doesn't count.) When tired, rest. When achy, move, stretch or rest. Crown your body Queen of Life, and serve it with reverence and faith. Trust that your body knows what it needs for its own sake and for the sake of your baby, and that it will let you know. All you have to do is listen willingly.

Time here is of the essence. Each day, spend a few minutes in quiet reflection and mindful appreciation of the miracles that occur inside of you. Fall in love with your body, for life, just as you imagine you will when you first lay eyes on your newborn babe. The thing about falling and being in love is that we always find time. It is not a matter of will, discipline or time management. It is a matter of inexhaustible desire.

Take interest in your body. Ask what it wants, and bless it with your caring answers. One day, in an unfathomably far away future, your baby will be grown up and make her own choices. You hope that she will make good ones. You will want her to know what you mean when you call after her: "Take care of yourself".

MATTER MINDS

I am in love with my body. (You probably guessed.) This wasn't always the case but pregnancy, birth and motherhood are good matchmakers. They hooked me up with my body and lobbied on its behalf, until I could not help but fall for it. It has been a love for life ever since.

The body knows things. With or without your conscious knowing, it moves you through life. It wakes you in the mornings, drives you places, sits you down and gets you up, lets you enjoy a good laugh, clean house, make repairs, puts you to sleep at night. It knows how to breathe, how to swallow, digest, protect, eliminate, repair, hear, and see; and it knows how to give birth. Menstruation, ovulation, conception, pregnancy, lactation and giving birth are natural functions of the female reproductive body. They happen, with few exceptions, on their own. You don't have to take classes or read books to make them happen. While it may be helpful and comforting to understand the physiological processes involved, you can't think or explain your way through pregnancy and birth. You can only go through it and let your body do what it knows best. To do this, you need to retire your thinking mind and trust a different set of brains: the chief commanders of your uterus, limbic system, and heart.

Giving up control and putting faith into your body may not be easy, especially when traveling unfamiliar terrain like childbirth. The body may be a marvelous thing, but it is dark and mysterious in there. It is no surprise we look to books and experts when preparing for birth. We look high and low and pretty much everywhere – except in one place: in our own bodies. High rates of medically augmented labors and of Cesarean sections are evidence for this confusion and testimony to a way of thinking that favors mind over matter, intellect over nature, doing over being. We believe birth can be managed with the right technology, the right intervention, the right breathing technique. Who needs the body?

But it is not that simple. A woman's body is not a machine. Our bodies are intelligent, complex systems, capable of processing and communicating vital information with us at all times. This is true whether we are awake or sleeping, listening to our bodies or not. Research in neuroscience and psychoneuroimmunology, the study of how mind and body interact, shows that the body is capable of storing memories in its cells. The body remembers when we didn't get enough sleep, when we sit hunched in front of the computer for hours, when we sugarcoat feelings of emptiness and pain. It remembers injury, maltreatment and ignorance. While the body may be silenced for the duration of labor or surgery, it can't be rendered oblivious. The concept "mind over matter" may be useful when we seek certainty and education, make plans, follow schedules, or invent our lives. But in birth we need to give voice to another player. We need to let our body mind its own business. It has its own intelligence, communicates and cares. Matter minds.

SURVIVAL

Matter minds because our body (matter) has one central agenda: to survive. Whether human, animal, microbial or plant, the body's main purpose is to be alive, to stay alive, to be functioning, and to be well. To be successful in this goal, the body attempts to carry out its various functions in a balanced fashion.

The state of balance within an organism and its tendency to maintain equilibrium is called homeostasis. Disturbances and disruptions of this internal equilibrium threaten the body in carrying out its mission and trigger adaptive responses to reinstate homeostasis. Acute or prolonged assaults on the body's effort to maintain equilibrium lead to internal dysregulation, distress, disease, and even death. This, our body is not okay with. While it will serve our needs and wishes, it will try to avoid self-annihilation.

The body's first duty is to life. Our body diligently records and communicates critical events and harmful experiences via physical sensations, moods, thoughts and behavioral symptoms. It will let us know when we are crossing bounds and need to start paying attention. If we don't, we may be in for an uncomfortable surprise. The body is not a quitter. It will continue to take note of unwholesome experiences, whether we have the time, desire or ability to notice them or not, and intensify the symptoms associated with the experience, just like an ink pen retracing a word increasingly saturates and deepens the print. Headaches become more frequent, pain more debilitating, depression more dismal, anger more uncontrollable.

Eventually we have to give in and acknowledge our body's attempts to get us on board with survival. We are wise to bow to its needs (or get on our knees and weep) and become the one who is taking orders.

MINDFULNESS

I've never been on an ocean cruise other than the voyage across birth. But if I'd ever make it onto the mighty waters of the world, I'd want to bring this: my ears and eyes. I'd want to hear the roar of the ocean and the wind breaking in my ears, and I'd want to see the stars. I'd want to lie on my back on rocking planks and look at the sky, aglow with millions of stars too fathomless to comprehend and dazzling in their temptation. I'd want to feel my breath, alive in the mystery of creation, and praise the intelligence behind it all with gladness. "How good – to be alive! How infinite – to be Alive – two-fold – The Birth I had – And this – besides, in – Thee!", acclaims Emily Dickinson. I can't think of a better song to salute the stars in my good fortune to know them. I can know them because I have eyes and ears that are mine to apply.

Our body is a gateway into the present. With it and through it we get to feel the heartbeat of creation, the miraculous, moment-to-moment unfolding of our personal history along the tangent of time. But this is only possible if we are mindfully aware of what is happening within our body's conceptual range.

Mindfulness is the conscious application of our senses to the present as it comes into existence from moment to moment. Each heart beat, breath or tickle we notice is part of a new moment which, barely discernible, gives way to other moments rich with novel impressions. Mindfulness fills the mind with what is happening in the here and now. The German word for "awareness", Wahrnehmung, captures this phenomena well. A compound word of *wahr* (meaning "true or truthful") and *nehmen* (meaning "to take or claim"), awareness is to claim the truth. This is an active, gradual, noble and mystifying process. How can we possibly comprehend what even one single moment is made of?

Our mind, governed by space and time, has considerable limitations when it comes to knowing what is true and real. Consider, for example, the following labor scenario: You are 35 weeks into your pregnancy when your water breaks one afternoon. Four hours later you start having contractions, and though you and your partner feel a bit startled and anxious that your baby is already coming, you settle into labor quite well. Several hours pass, night is falling, and the next day is approaching. In the early morning hours, your labor is picking up, and you feel increasing pressure in your pelvis. You ask your midwives to check your cervical dilation who tell you that you are fully dilated. With renewed energy, you begin to push. Things go well for a couple of hours, but into your third hour of pushing, your contractions are becoming increasingly painful. You are struggling to keep your spirits up and the pain at bay. You notice that your body hurts, you are tired, and your mind is racing as you are trying to make sense of what is going on. You may be worried about your baby, think that he is stuck, and fast forward to the possibility of a C-section. Much to your dismay, you can't figure out what is happening. This is a rather scary proposition because you (and your body) want your baby to be safe. On high alert, mind comes up with all kinds of explanations, and some of them may feel like the truth. However, your thoughts are only a fraction of what is true in each moment; they are not the truth.

Buddhism doesn't make a distinction between body and mind, affording the body as much capacity for knowing truth as the mind. Thoughts are nothing but a function of the mind, just like hearing is a function of the ear, and smelling a function of the nose. The mind is simply another sense organ, nothing more special than say the tongue. Neither does it have any unusual privileges. Thoughts are transient sensations, just like the sensations of sound, vision, smell, taste and touch. While they are certainly worth noticing, they don't hold the monopoly on accurate, intelligent reflection of reality. I find this understanding helpful. I don't have to be the victim of my wits and whims, and can take liberty in trusting other sources of wisdom. Practicing mindfulness, I gently put my thoughts back into their place. I harness their eagerness and line them up with my other senses. And something magical happens: my thoughts begin to settle. They become all eyes and ears, calling my mind into the witness stand of lived experience.

BACK TO THE BODY

This witness stand is our body. Everything we feel and call life plays on this stage. And how much is going on there! Take labor and birth alone. Hormones are produced and excreted in the right amount and at the right time; tissues stretch while others contract; oxygen is metabolized into glucose and muscle energy. While many of these processes are impossible to witness (at least for most of us), others can be made aware. Placing mindful attention on your body's sensations in labor is ground-breaking. It pulls you into the changeable, transient here and now, moving you along with the swiftness of water.

To mammals, birth is just that: a slow effacing call from within the body's cave, carrying in its echo the memory of creation. If you have watched an animal give birth, you may have seen how the mother knew what to do at various stages in her labor. She listens and knows how to breathe, how to position herself, and how to move. Her only agenda is to execute the ancient script of birthing.

Think of labor as the time to read this script. Think of it as reading a good novel. As you turn, with each contraction, page after page, you start to comprehend the story. You start to notice details and patterns, and it all starts to make sense.

The yin-yang symbol offers a helpful metaphor for understanding the role of body and mind in labor. Look at the yin-yang symbol on the next page and imagine that one half represents labor and the other half represents your day-to-day life. White (yang) symbolizes mind, black (yin) symbolizes the body. Which half do you think stands for labor?

When I ask this question in my classes, most couples point to the darker side as the body takes center stage when a woman goes into labor. The mind serves as a reflective audience, a strong beam of light capable of illuminating our body's experience.

WHAT ABOUT PAIN?

For ages, pregnancy and birth have been the sacred work of women. Your body has been given the seed of your baby. In silent and spectacular ways it has known how to grow this seed into a fetus. It knew how to sculpt the chambers of your baby's heart and the folds of her brain, and how to orchestrate the formation of her limbs, internal organs and spine. Your body has done all this work entirely on its own. There was nothing *you* had to do. Your body knew what to do when, in what order, and in what time – because it recognized the seed of your baby as a gift of Life itself. Your body takes this endowment seriously, all the way through pregnancy, and when the time comes to release it. Your body wants to give birth, and it will do anything to accomplish its sacred mission. Labor pain is part of this design.

It is important to note upfront that labor pain is not by nature pathological. While labor and childbirth are intense physical events for a woman, they are healthy and life-affirming processes, designed to bring forth life and to give mother and child a chance to pace themselves while doing the hard work of laboring. Contractions are usually under a minute long, followed by a respite three to four times their length to let mother and child recover. The physical sensations of labor and birth are agents of this process; they carry out the mission of Birth. It is an important mission, and the agents are powerful. They will demand all of your attention.

Almost nothing gets our attention as instantly as pain. If the body perceives actual or potential harm to itself, it will elicit pain to make sure we take action to get away from danger and injury. The body uses foolproof physiological signals to alert us to seek safety. Pain is one such primal signal. When we get hurt, thermal, mechanical and chemical pain receptors are stimulated and trigger autonomic nervous system responses which result in the experience of pain. This mobilizes us to look after the source of the pain so that our bodies can go on living.

While normal labor pain is not the product of perceived danger, it serves the same purpose to mobilize mothers to act in ways that ensure the survival of their young and the survival of our species. Mothers are often guided by pain to seek quiet and safety. By going inward, they can gather maximum focus for labor and birth, moving in accord with their body's command to be more comfortable, to minimize pain, and to effectively support the baby's descent. Positions that make use of gravity, allow the pelvis to move freely and encourage deep breathing facilitate this effort and can make labor pain manageable. This, at least, is the experience of many women. But what about mothers who claim they didn't experience any pain whatsoever? Their stories support the widely researched concept of pain as perception.

Our perceptions, or what we believe to be true, are influenced by subconscious and conscious processes such as emotions, memories and expected outcomes. In labor, they are also affected by the availability or lack of support. Studies have shown that mothers feel less labor pain when they are supported by people they trust and love. Similarly, people's experience of pain decreases when they connect with their pain through non-judgmental awareness, positive association or prayer. To me, this makes a lot of sense. If a woman in labor turns toward her body's sensations instead of away from it, her body is getting the attention it needs and doesn't have to fight for it. Does that mean we can make labor pain disappear with just the right methods?

As a first time pregnant mother, I liked to believe this to be true. I loved the idea of painless childbirth. Why would I not? Have my baby, and have him without pain? You bet! But my wishful thinking didn't get me far. Labor hurt, a lot. Contractions are all-consuming, full-body earthquakes. They are meant to open the new mother's body, mind and heart so that her baby can be born. This is radical work. Opening is hard, and often plain painful. What does it take to open up our body? How do we open our mind and heart?

For our body to be able to open, it needs to feel safe. Safety is also the most basic need for a mother in labor. Feeling things she's never felt before, experiencing pain, being physically exposed and not in control can be very scary.

It is a vulnerable proposition only a safe surrounding can remediate. Calm voices, warmth, privacy, and the company of people she loves and trusts can make the laboring mother feel safe. But her sense of safety does not only depend on her external environment. It is also influenced by her internal perceptions. She needs to feel safe with *herself*. If a laboring mother feels inadequate, pressured to perform, immodest or shameful, her body may not feel particularly excited about opening up. Self-judgment and negative self-beliefs are powerful inhibitors.

The American psychologist Abraham Maslow identified several human needs that build on our physiological and safety needs. Not only do we have a need for shelter, security and protection, but also for:

- friendship
- intimacy
- family
- affection
- companionship
- acceptance
- strength
- competence
- mastery
- self-confidence

- independence
- freedom
- respect
- autonomy
- dignity
- creativity
- tolerance
- spontaneity
- self-expression and
- self-acceptance.

Labor and birth make no exception.

Have another look at the above list of needs. Which ones stand out for you? Which ones do you think will be important for you in labor? A better understanding of your personal needs can help you identify which ones may serve you, or not, in labor. With my first labor, competence and self-confidence were very important to me. I needed to feel that I knew what I was doing, and that I was doing it well. But as contractions became more intense, I was less able to handle them. Beseeched by self-judgment, my sense of self-confidence, smug and gratified only hours earlier, shattered in its wake.

With my second and third baby, I voted for a different need. I practiced self-acceptance. Was labor less painful? Yes. Was it painless? No. Birth is intense no matter what, and the notion of pain is quite fitting. Even with an open mind, there is still the physical reality of your body stretching to let your baby pass through.

The uterus is a powerful muscle and, at the end of your pregnancy, quite big. When it contracts during labor, it exerts tremendous pressure on your cervix, back, groin, belly, bladder and bowels. To give you a sense of why contractions are painful, try to squeeze one of your hands into a fist really hard for about 45 seconds. Then multiply the size of your fist several times to get to the size of your full-term uterus and increase the amount of pressure by several pounds. The stretching of your cervix, vagina and pelvic floor is no small matter either. Perineal massage or deep forward bends in yoga are great ways to experience what it feels like when parts of your body are stretching. It gives you also an opportunity to rehearse strategies for being with discomfort in labor.

Breathe, relax your jaw and shoulders, and try to stay with your body's sensation without reacting to it. You don't have to be comfortable or like it; just be there with it to your best ability. Let your body get all your attention. When your baby is coming, pay attention to the messages your body is sending you. Your body wants you to hear them because it wants you and your baby be well. Listen to them all, in the full range of their intensity. Labor pain is not a punishment or inconvenience but a powerful blessing. It blesses mothers in three ways: it is transient, transformational, and transcending.

1. Labor pain is transient because, unlike other pain, contractions don't last very long. They come and go. Contractions build gradually, allowing the mother to find her rhythm and adjust to the work of birthing.
2. Labor pain is transformational. When you enter labor for the first time, you are a virgin to Birth, and when you have gone through it, you are born a mother.
3. Labor pain transcends space and time. Many mothers lose track of time in labor, and some have spiritual experiences of oneness and bliss.

This may or may not be your experience and has nothing to do with personal inadequacy or failure. Remember: Birth is bigger than you are. She will take you to the perfect place of your transformation. New mothers often put tremendous pressure on themselves when they prepare for birth, during birth, and after their baby is born (especially if the birth didn't go the way they had hoped). Birth becomes a battle field from which they are only allowed to return with the Natural Birth Badge of Honor. But birth is not a test. It is a gift, regardless of whether labor is painful, blissful, or something else.

The best gifts are the ones we receive unexpected and with open minds. So it goes with birth. Wait for the gift, instead of asking for what you want. Let go of expectations. Pay attention to what you believe or disbelieve about birth. Smile at your efforts to make sense of something that cannot yet be known. Let labor begin and settle in the muscles, organs and joints of your body. Wait to see what contractions feel like, and where they are going. Listen to the story they have to tell. Be the perfect audience. Follow each contraction to the beginning, the middle, and the end; and then do it again. A rose is a rose is a rose.

Practice non-attached awareness. If your personal perception of labor includes the vocabulary of pain, so be it. Let the pain be a rose. Smell it, touch it, and behold it in its glory. Mindfulness and pain are powerful partners. If labor is something other than pain, let that be too. Follow its calling. Let it be intensity, wildness, power, stillness, emptiness or bliss, and move on, no strings attached. During my second and third labor there were stretches of time when I did not feel pain – though I noticed all kinds of intense and crazy sensations. But pain did not register as a concept. Whatever I felt was beyond cognition, suspended in the pre-verbal plasma of my body. I could have called it "pain" if someone had asked me. But no one did, and pain did not occur to me. Until I was afraid.

WORKING WITH FEAR

When fear enters labor, all bets are off. Contractions often come closer together, become longer or more spaced out, and are almost always more painful. Fear in labor begets pain. This pain is unlike any other, a tireless and unyielding force mothers often don't escape short of medical intervention. And there is a reason for this pain. In birth we need to open, but when there is fear the opposite happens: Our body contracts and attempts to close up. As the vehicle of Birth, it is trapped. Birth demands: Open! Fear howls: No! Stay on guard!

This is madness for the body. Confused and alarmed, it turns up the volume of pain. Listen!, body implores, This is not working! Stop what you are doing! It's not safe!

A mother's body is uncompromising when it comes to birth. It will try anything to ensure the safe arrival of her baby. If needed, extreme pain will do. Extreme pain exposes fear's hidden power and urges us to face our fears by putting up flares in the dark so we know where to look. But we don't always look. We may be unwilling, feel too vulnerable, unsupported or too afraid to look. Sometimes it's easier to endure pain than to face our fears. Until desperation gives us the impetus for courage, or we take deliberate steps ahead of time to explore and clear potential fears. Journaling, counseling, or other forms of self-inquiry are helpful here.

During my first labor, it took me long and painful hours to admit I was afraid. I couldn't even admit I was in pain. Plain overwhelmed, I tried to absorb the pain of my body in the folds of delusion. But when my voice gave in and I could scream no longer, I committed myself to the pain. I accepted I was afraid and needed help. This was a turning point. I aligned myself with Birth and took the necessary steps to work again with my body. I asked for an epidural, and dilated within two hours from three to ten centimeters. When I had stopped fighting the contractions (and telling my body No!), my body quickly and efficiently resumed the work of opening. I could almost hear it sigh with relief.

If you experience unbearable pain in labor, ask yourself whether you are afraid. Try to share your experience with someone you love and trust. Give yourself permission to speak or cry or rage about it. Whatever you choose, listen to your pain and let it speak. Whether your pain tells you that you are afraid of the next contraction, disappointed in yourself, or doubtful about being a mother, trust it and give it voice. It is relevant! Not only will this help you move forward in labor and help your birth team better support you, it will help your baby too.

Most fears that come up for mothers during labor are psychological in nature. But whether irrational or real, fear triggers the same physiological responses in our body. With predictable precision, our body releases legions of adrenaline, cortisol and other stress hormones to prepare us to fight or flight. Remember, it believes it is under threat. And here is the catch: our body keeps up this preparation unless we do something about it. Like good sentinels, our nervous and endocrine systems raise a ruckus until help arrives to restore safety and order. Exercising, sweating, talking, screaming, crying, and deep breathing are helpful and healthy ways to metabolize high levels of adrenaline and lower toxic stress. Changing positions, moving about or dancing to a recording of drums can help as well.

If none of this helps, go into your pain. Assess whether there is any real danger to you or your baby. Have your midwife or doctor check your baby's heart rate and positioning. If there is evidence for potential harm, take appropriate action. But if your and your baby's well-being is confirmed and your pain is still unbearable, ask yourself: Do I feel safe? Is there something I am afraid of? Anything that doesn't feel right about my surroundings, the smell, the lighting, the people in the room? Anything I am at odds with in myself? What is in the way?

Go within, and share what you find. Fear loses its power when we find the courage to call it out. Whisper your fear into someone's ear. Yell it out loud. Bear it witness. Know your fear, and then give it away. If your fear and pain still don't make sense, accept that things are not always conclusive or under our control. Have compassion for yourself and for the choices that may come out of the situation — whether this is a transfer to the hospital, an epidural, or a delivery in the OR. Do what you can to stay grounded and present. This birth, just like your baby, is a gift, and you will have time to claim it.

WHAT IF...

Your body knows how to give birth. Birth is a gift you will have time to claim.

I don't write this light-heartedly. It is an easy thing to say if labor goes smoothly, and mother and child are well. But this doesn't always happen. Sometimes things go wrong. This is an uneasy thought. You may not want to go there, and if that's the case, feel free to skip this section. Some cultures and people believe that it is harmful for a pregnant mother to think or talk about fears or painful birth outcomes. Instead, mothers are encouraged to think only positive thoughts and surround themselves with affirming stories. Otherwise, the unthinkable may come true.

While I love affirmations and positive thinking (and believe they are powerful), I don't think they necessarily get us what we want or make us immune against the things we don't want. Life and birth are not always under our control, and our conventional mind is limited in its ability to attract desired outcomes. Therefore, examining our fears beforehand can be empowering and liberating. It also allows us to do some contingency planning and can, in effect, reduce the impact of a traumatic event, should it occur. Courtney Jarecki and Laurie Perron Mednick, fellow Portland birth professionals, have championed research and advocacy for Cesarean preparedness and written a book about it[3]. They have found that women who prepare for the possibility of a Cesarean birth have a less traumatic experience if their natural birth dream ends in this way.

The great majority of labors end with a healthy baby and mother, but complications happen. Despite the best of preparations, some labors are very long, require transfers to the hospital, emergency C-sections, forceps deliveries. Babies are born prematurely or with birth defects. Babies die. Does that mean that the body failed? That it can't be trusted after all?

After I had my first two children I became pregnant with a third. Nine weeks later I miscarried. I buried the body of this baby, already fully recognizable with its ten fingers and toes, under the old plum tree in our backyard. In the weeks and months that followed, I tried to make sense of what had happened. I had had two successful pregnancies before, and was healthy and young. It did not make sense that my body did not comply. What was wrong with it? Adding to my confusion, I kept bleeding for weeks. I started

---

3   Courtney K. Jarecki, *Homebirth Cesarean: Stories and Support for Families and Healthcare Providers* (Portland: Incisio Press, 2015).

acupuncture to stop the flow. One day I started sobbing on the acupuncture table. The needles burnt like stroked matches under my skin as I shook with grief, and all was pain. I cried for this lost baby. I did not know who this baby was, whether girl or boy, or why it had come and gone. I was overwhelmed with sorrow for this unknown soul, and for this unknown soul I wept. Not for me and my own unfulfilled desires, but for this nameless child. And my grief made sense.

Our body's central agenda (to survive and to live) aligns with one other, greater desire: to be of service to the soul. Bodies live, and bodies die in active duty to our soul's journey. The journey of our soul is not always obvious, but the body often shows us the way. Physical sensations, pain, illness, injury, loss, or strong attraction are the visible foot prints of our soul. Our bodies want what our souls want, whether that is what our ego wants or not. Our ego may want to control the body and everything else for that matter (I did not want to lose this baby), but our body remains faithful to the soul. "[The body] is only interested in our growing into a deeper, more complete, embodied, and authentic way of being," writes meditation teacher Reggie Ray[4]. "And this is where the process becomes extremely personal, very challenging, and sometimes quite painful."

Not only is this process deeply personal but so are our attempts to make sense of it. We all need to find our own meaning as our body carries us along. My miscarriage offered me a glimpse into the heart of my soul, and from this I coined meaning. Grieving the baby I had lost, I took comfort in the thought that the soul of this child just needed a mother to grieve her. Maybe no one had grieved for this soul, ever. Maybe it was never missed, never loved, and needed to follow a journey of its own.

Finding this meaning let me grieve willingly. It was healing. Where there had been disappointment and hurt pride, there now was only Love. There have been other times in my life when my soul called on her faithful servant, my body. Pregnancy and birth were prime events, but so were major illnesses, meeting my husband, falling in love, losing loved ones. Following my body's current in joy and grief, whether of my choosing or not, I was always guided to Love, and to love more deeply than I had known. Maybe the soul is nothing other than Love. And the body is her devoted lover.

---

4   Reginald A. Ray, *Touching Enlightenment: Finding Realization in the Body* (Louisville: Sounds True, 2014), 184.

FIFTY WAYS TO LOVE YOUR BODY

1 Take a foot bath 2 Stand under a warm shower 3 Massage your belly 4 Adorn your body with henna 5 Roll around the floor 6 Make a healthy meal just for yourself 7 Watch the sunrise 8 Sing 9 Get a haircut 10 Receive a massage 11 Walk barefoot in grass 12 Go to the playground and sit on a swing 13 Put your legs up on a wall 14 Take a candlelight bath 15 Sit down to eat 16 Eat slowly 17 Lie on the grass 18 Drink tea while it's still hot 19 Gaze at the clouds 20 Take a walk in nature 21 Put new sheets on your bed 22 Take a nap 23 Apply essential oils to your skin 24 Step outside 25 Breathe 26 Sit straight 27 Smell a flower 28 Rest your eyes on the horizon 29 Lift your face up to the rain 30 Smile 31 Get up and stretch 32 Eat chocolate 33 Make love 34 Grow a garden 35 Twirl 36 Go upside down 37 Have a good cry 38 Walk slowly 39 Play tickle games 40 Go to bed early 41 Sweat 42 Hug somebody you love 43 Arrange flowers in a vase 44 Sleep under the stars 45 Make a belly cast 46 Spend a day in silence 47 Watch the sunset 48 Bless your food 49 Drink water 50 Rustle through fallen leaves.

A MOVIE STAR'S DILEMMA

And so you begin. You are more mindful of your relationship with your body and are taking better care of it. You understand that you are as much in service to your body as it is to you. So far so good. But what about your mind? Can you love and care for it just as much?

Mind certainly is magical. Like a movie star, it is popular, glamorous and often entertaining. We are drawn to it and want what it promises to have: vitality, money, smarts, fame and power. Glowing skin, no stretchmarks, and a sexy belly. The birth suite with the jacuzzi. The answer to all our questions. We adore and study it on glossy pages. Mind gives our striving purpose and direction. It makes us follow our dreams, get an education, build a profession, plant gardens, pursue relationships. But like all movie stars, mind walks around in sweats after the cameras are packed away and everyone goes home. When no one is watching, it is just as conventional as anything. It knows boredom, jealousy and fear. The room with the jacuzzi is taken. The promises don't hold and, disillusioned, we turn away. What to do? How can we understand this brilliant star?

Our love-hate relationship with the mind is the result of a misunderstanding, brought about by the mind itself. Eager to make sense of the world, mind tries to get us through the day. It ponders and calculates, conceptualizes and judges, and in doing so gives rise to this and that, now and then, you and me. These dualities are reinforced by emotions which further consolidate the version (a-version) we have of ourselves and the world.

But this is not all there is to the mind. Yoga sages and Buddhist masters speak of a different mind. They call it a shining jewel, pure and clear. We all have it, they say, but it is hidden from view. What we see instead, and believe to be real, are the things it reflects. Imagine standing by a mountain lake. On a clear calm day, you may see the surrounding trees, mountain tops and sky reflected in the water. But the reflections are not the lake. They are part of the lake's capacity to mirror. Now throw a big stone into the lake. The surface of the lake will break into countless ripples, each reflecting a different fragment of what moments before was more coherent and smooth. You see light images and dark ones, shapes and shapeless impressions, and are fascinated by the ever changing display of colors and appearances.

We feel the same way about our mind. We usually believe that our thoughts, emotions and sensory perceptions are the real deal. We get caught up in their compelling nature, and fail to behold the shining jewel of our mind. Like the spikes of a fast-moving wheel, our mental ripples spin around a still point of cosmic size, but all we can see is the spinning.

This flurry is dependent upon its physiological basis, our brain. In the human species, brain and mind are inseparably linked. Any sensory stimulus we experience —the cry of a baby, the smell of lavender, the feeling of a contraction— follows the neuronal traffic rules of our brain. After our body receives a stimulus, chemical messengers send a signal to the thalamus and the limbic system. It is within those brain structures that our nervous system decides if a sensory stimulus is safe, dangerous, or none of the two, kind of like an omnipotent mother who decrees what is good or bad for her adolescent child. Once the limbic brain has put a sticky note of emotional priority to a specific signal, it passes this information to the neocortex. This is where the fun begins.

For example, lets say a pacifier moves into your field of vision. Up until this point, the pacifier is nothing but a circular shaped object. At the limbic level, it is flagged as good, bad or neutral — depending on your past experiences with this object. Your neocortex takes this information to town. It seeks and volunteers all kinds of gossip about the initial stimulus: Silicone pacifiers are better than latex ones Pacifiers are a waste of money Always buy a half dozen Make sure you wean by age two.

Welcome to the monkey mind. Our neocortex is the jungle gym of the monkey mind. It provides us with non-stop entertainment. It gives us characters and props, sound-track and dialog. We shall never be bored. But what is it that we are watching? Is it real? When we rewind the thought manufacturing process and go back, step by step, to where a thought was born, routing back to the limbic system, back to the thalamus, back to the sensory nerves and all the way back to the object, we are left with little. A circular shape, a fragrance, a reflection of light. Raw experience. What is a thought? The result of brain function, mental process. A perception. A designation of meaning. A judgment and choice. A constructed image. Pattern matching and recognition.

There is nothing wrong with the way the mind works. The mind cares. It is useful, sharp and brilliant. It just gets carried away. Uneasy with the unknown, our mind is the Sherlock Holmes of our unfulfilled desires. Always looking for explanations, resolutions, the way out, it gets excited when there is something to solve. That's its job! To the mind the whole world is a riddle. Intrigued with itself, clouds are not just clouds but shapes of mythical creatures or a precursor for rain. A traffic jam is not just a traffic jam but a nuisance or an obstacle. A labor contraction is not just a contraction but a challenge or concern. What if it gets worse? What if something is wrong?

Seeing the mind as it is, not as it parades to be seen takes dilligence and discernment. But when we can see our thoughts for what they are – spinning tales of whimsical power – we can look at the clouds and see ... clouds. We can be in labor and feel ... the body giving birth.

THE AFFIRMATION DILEMMA

The goal of yoga is to calm the mind so that it returns to its original, undisturbed state. The ripples on the lake recede, the cast out stone reverses direction as it breaks the surface of the lake, and returns into your hand. The images of trees, mountain tops and sky congeal into a cohesive whole. The lake is still. You stand by the lake. And that's all there is. There are no words or commentaries. The mind is quiet and keen in its perception. It doesn't need a voiceover to behold the perfection of this moment.

And yet, without practice, it does. Habitually and often. Mind likes something to comment on, often with the best of intentions. This is when mind resorts to soothing self-talk, prayer or affirmations. Now, I love and use them all, especially affirmations. I use them frequently and with deliberation. Some are posted at various places in my home, some I divine as needed with the help of sacred texts and affirmations cards. Affirmations are my restart button when I feel off center, incompetent as a parent, vulnerable, or plain stupid. A good affirmation at the right time can do wonders for the fretful soul!

But affirmations have their limits. They are not a magic bullet. They can miss the point by miles and leave us just as bewildered as before, especially when what we are trying to affirm is a wildly moving target. Repeating to myself "I am calm" when I'm upset or anxious, or "I'm relaxed" when my body is gripped with pain, is at minimum a joke. Who am I kidding?!

Affirmations are very popular to use in labor. And by all means, use them. But don't count on them getting you through it because they may not. Birth will challenge any self-induced hypnosis. Yogi Paramahansa Yogananda, who has perfected the science of affirmation all his life, tells us that affirmations fail because we get distracted and lack "soul conviction"[5]. Affirmations turn to "husks without corn" because our mind is fickle and unsteady in its faith and focus. If you are drawn to affirmations as you prepare for birth and want to use them, take his advice to heart. Believe, with utter conviction, in the power of your affirmation, and meditate on it daily.

This reminds me of a German fairy tale. As a child I was fascinated by the story of a golden goose that had the power to glue everyone who touched it to the person who touched the goose last. Being golden and all, it didn't take long for the goose to have a long trail of wayward followers. Problem was, the peasants, musicians and maids had to go along with the goose wherever it wanted. When they gave into their temptation to touch the shiny thing, they lost their freedom and power. To me, thoughts are like the golden goose. Here comes a thought, we have the desire to touch it, and soon we'll wander off with it. Where to, we rarely know.

But there is one more piece to the story. There was one person who could touch the goose without being bound to it, a young, unassuming shoemaker named Hans. Kindhearted, cheerful and somewhat simple, Hans had but one goal: to take the goose to the king's castle to make the princess laugh. No one had been able to cheer the princess up, and in his good heart Hans could not bear to see her suffer. When he found the goose, he marched off to bring it to the princess. He had Yogananda's soul conviction, and nothing could deter or distract him. Focusing on his one and only thought –The princess shall be happy– he thus succeeded and made her laugh (and everyone lived happily ever after).

As the tale and I suggest, our mind likes to follow shiny, novel things, whether that's a golden goose, a physical sensation, a thought, an attraction. If you have tried to meditate you probably know how much the mind likes to wander. Regardless how much we focus on our breath or another meditation

---

5 Paramahansa Yogananda, *Scientific Healing Affirmations* (Los Angeles: Self-Realization Fellowship, 2007), 3-16.

object (a mantra, affirmation, particular sensation), the mind is often restless and unwilling to stay put. It wants to check out other golden geese. While it is entertaining and not without merit to wander off with our thoughts, they often lead us astray. They are like snow falling from the sky, appearing in rapid succession out of seemingly empty space. We have to be diligent in our focus to avoid getting lost. This is especially true for labor.

Labor and birth are physically stormy events, and the strength of affirmations must match the power of contractions. This is a tall order. Other thoughts and fears (this is harder than I thought... how much longer is it gonna be...) may compete for your attention, not to mention the strong physical sensations of labor. It may not be easy to stay tuned into affirmation station. Now what?

Yoga is about the now and the what. It calls us to stop, rest our case, and notice what is happening in front of us. We lift our face to the sky. We feel the wet kisses of snow on our cheeks and hear the silent blessing of white blankets. We enter the kingdom of Now.

THE KINGDOM OF NOW

The kingdom of Now has countless chambers. Contrary to affirmations which reserve exclusive attention to only one "thought chamber", yoga hands you a telescope to the spectacle of your lived experience. Yoga shows you the turning sky of all that is Now – thoughts, feelings, sensations, and all that is knowable in one moment.

Let's take this "moment" for example. I am working on this book. It is Sunday morning. I feel fullness in my belly. Memory of breakfast ten minutes ago. My son walks in the room, looks for something. He walks out of the room. Another moment. Tea down my throat. Lingering spice on warm tongue. Honey down my throat. Fingers resting on the keyboard. Resting. Quiet cove of body and breath. Crossed legs, left knee on top of right, soles of feet open and cold. The phone rings. Am I going to answer or not? It still rings. It stops. Is this still the same moment? Or the next? How can I know?

Back to the body. The open book of my eyes, ears, nose, tongue, skin. Sitting up. Shoulders down my back. Glaring at the computer screen. Here goes the phone again. Again! On Sunday morning! Footsteps down the hallway, my younger daughter running to answer the phone. She can't find it. Comes charging into the room. I get up and help her find it. Does that count for a moment? I'm not sure.

I am trying to stay in the moment, and the moment keeps playing peek-a-boo. Now it walks into the room as my son. Now it itches on my face. Making me scratch. My arms getting cold. More tea would be nice. I get up and make more tea. Fill the kettle with water. Turn the kettle on. Back to the computer. Waiting. Waiting for the next moment to reveal itself.

Here it comes, disguised as my daughter peeking into the room to share a favorite song with me. Makes me smile. The water is boiling. I go and pour my tea. Read the label on the tea bag: "I shut my eyes in order to see. ~Paul Gauguin". I shut my eyes. Upper eye lid meeting lower eye lid. Typing the words without looking. (Will correct typos later.) The ears take over. Laughter in the kitchen. A door closing. Little feet dancing. A car driving by outside. The road still slick with rain. Tires dragging a watery tail. Where is it going? I open my eyes. A dizzying merry-go-round of brilliant moments. Here one instant, and gone the next.

Yoga reminds us that no experience is fixed in time and space. Everything is changeable and actively changing, including our body, thoughts, beliefs, or sense of self. The same is true for labor. Contractions are not only different in the beginning of labor than toward the end, they are also different when they are about to start, build, peak, release, or fade away. Pay attention to those changes from moment to moment, and open to the fluid unfolding of birth. Unhitch from the gravitational pull of your desires, and be free to appreciate what is yours to receive.

Liberation

My eyes already touch the sunny hill,
going far ahead of the road I have begun.
So we are grasped by what we cannot grasp;
it has inner light, even from a distance –
and changes us, even if we do not reach it,
into something else, which, hardly sending it,
we already are.

~Rainer Maria Rilke

From the moment we are born, we have needs. We need warmth, skin contact, food, shelter, and a place next to a beating heart. As we grow and the circle of our reach increases, our needs amplify paralleled by the wants and desires of our emerging ego. Soon, they suffuse every waking moment until the day we die.

This is the story of our lives. We are creatures of the earth, dependent on our body's needs for survival and desire for comfort and pleasure. This also sets us up for suffering. We can't have one without the other, are hopelessly caught between the polarities of pleasure and pain. Or can we?

People have searched, since the beginning of time, for ways to transcend our lamentable limitations. They have gone on pilgrimages and sat, unmoving, under ancient trees. They have prayed in cloister cells and dungeons, burned and smoked sacred herbs, fasted, sacrificed, built temples, retreated to the desert and to remote mountain caves. Their efforts to be free from suffering typically focused on the body, often to the point of self-abnegation.

The Buddha, in his desire to understand and transcend the causes of suffering, almost died trying. After years of starving himself, a village maid found him sitting, mere skin and bones, under a banyan tree. She had prepared a milk pudding to bring as an offering to a tree deity she had prayed to in hope of bearing a son. When she saw the Buddha, she thought he was the god who lived in the tree. The Buddha may or may not have known about her intention, but he was moved by her kindness and accepted her gift. He realized, in that moment, that forsaking the body is not the way to freedom. Flooded with compassion for himself and all of life, he renounced his ascetic ways and found enlightenment that very night.

Compassion for our body and respect for life have become the key teachings of the Buddha. They are also the key teachings of classical yoga. Whether they afford us enlightenment the way the Buddha has known is not the point. A life governed by love, courage, curiosity and kindness is. These are some of the practices that pave the way to liberation. Love liberates from clinging, courage from fear, curiosity from indifference, kindness from spite and ill will. The following chapter contemplates practices I have found most helpful in labor and life. Think of them as playing *with* an instrument. Playing with an instrument is different than playing it. It leaves room for experiment and improvisation, trial and error. Don't get hung up on technique. Explore and remember to have fun.

ARRIVING

Yoga begins with arriving. The moment you get off the mental roller coaster of your daily agendas, unplug from the stream of sensory stimulations, release expectations, and pause just long enough to experience yourself as more than your strivings and imperfections, you make contact with yoga. This is the beauty of it. You don't need to roll out a yoga mat to open the door to liberation. Neither do you need to make special arrangements for Birth. Your open-hearted presence is enough.

Years ago, when I was new to yoga, I asked my teacher whether she practiced yoga every day. "I am", she said, "but I am not doing poses every day." I was surprised to hear this but did not know what to make of it. How could you do yoga without practicing on the mat? Too awed and shy I didn't ask my teacher but knew, when I learned about the yamas and niyamas, the ten ethical precepts of yoga, that I had found an answer. I felt also relief. After I had my baby it had become challenging to make it to yoga class. Often weeks went by without going to the studio. I felt bad about this because I questioned my commitment to yoga. Going to class equaled practicing equaled being a true yogini. And if I wasn't going to class I was clearly a fraud.

The yamas and niyamas became my saving grace. Attending a yoga class is not the yard stick that measures a new mother's sincerity as a yogini. What matters is her daily commitment to unplug, pause, and become aware, at any moment, anywhere. Motherhood will provide you with countless opportunities to practice. Sitting quietly while nursing your baby, eating slowly, or striving to be more patient are equal to sitting in lotus pose. Staying calm after being woken by a crying baby for the fourth time in the night matches any handstand, and breathing deeply when your nerves are on fire any hamstring stretch.

FOUNDATIONS

The yamas and niyamas are the true North of my practice. They keep me oriented and on track when life gets too busy to practice on the mat. The yamas (non-violence, truthfulness, non-stealing, restraint, non-grasping) remind us how to be in good relationship with others, i.e. friends, family members, neighbors, animals, the earth, and, if you are pregnant, with the baby you are carrying.

The niyamas (purity, contentment, self-discipline, self-study, surrender) are about right conduct with yourself, including your thoughts, feelings, body, and the yearnings of your soul.

Ahimsa : Non-violence

Ahimsa is the bedrock of yogic conduct. We are to approach others with a spirit of peacefulness, kindness and compassion, and avoid actions that could hurt another being. Most pregnant mothers I have worked with are very concerned about the well-being of their unborn child. They don't smoke, drink or eat junk food to excess as this may harm their baby. But what about holding grudges, blaming others or putting yourself down? Negative thoughts and critical remarks can hurt deeply. Ahimsa is not an easy principle to practice; I find it to be one of the most challenging. It requires compassion, forgiveness and ongoing vigilance.

Labor and birth add a unique dimension to this. You want a healthy baby and the natural birth that supports this outcome. But what if things don't go as smoothly as hoped? How do you know which choices are the least harmful?

Education about labor drugs and interventions can give you partial answers. But we often don't know how our actions affect others (or your baby) until after the fact. Sometimes all we can do is trust that we do the right thing, and that in itself is the most compassionate choice in the moment.

Today, ask yourself: Am I making healthy choices? Do my actions and choices bring more peace or more conflict into the world? Am I kind to others and to myself? What is the most compassionate response in this moment?

Satya : Truthfulness

Satya is about speaking and living truthfully. At a very basic level, this means we don't tell lies or mislead others. On a more subtle level, satya commands us a) to find our own truth and b) to act on its behest. This is not always easy. You may not trust yourself, or confuse someone else's truth with your own. Maybe you have wanted to work with a home birth midwife, but family members and friends have cautioned and convinced you that giving birth in the hospital is safer and better. Maybe you want to wean your baby by six months so you can go back to work full-time, but go on breastfeeding (and pumping) because that's what everyone else in your community does.

Our truth often changes over time. But often it doesn't, and what was once true will stand the test of time. It takes conscience, trust and solitude to find our truth. And heart to speak it.

The truth is not always popular. Sometimes it is easier to consent to social, cultural or family pressure than to do what is right for us. But here is the good news: Labor and birth are great opportunities to follow your truth. How you go through labor is truly up to you, and there is no right or wrong way of doing it.

In our birth classes we encourage mothers and their partners to find out what may be working for them best instead of telling them what to do. We don't prescribe pain coping techniques. We let them explore options. If they are drawn to the breath, so be it. If they'd rather do times tables, more power to them. One mom told us triumphantly she muttered the word "motherf*****" under her breath when she was in labor, and she had the birth she had wanted.

Today, ask yourself: Does the birth class I signed up for feel right to me? Does it get me closer to finding the truth about myself as a laboring woman? Do I feel good about my choice of midwife/doctor/doula? Who did I invite to my baby's birth, and why? What are my motivations? Do they still work for me?

Asteya : Non-stealing

Asteya asks us to leave what doesn't belong to us. This applies to other people's possessions, personal space, time and process. We respect that everyone has their own thoughts, feelings, needs and desires. When we talk to others, we hear what they have to say. We don't demand, interrupt, manipulate or coerce based on feelings of entitlement or power. Many women write up a birth plan and become very attached to it. But labor doesn't always start and go as planned. Babies may have their plan too, including when they are ready to be born. Pushing baby's arrival with an early induction or scheduled Cesarean (unless medically indicated) may interfere with important psychospiritual processes and baby's maturation in the womb. In labor, ask your baby what she may want. Try to respect how her labor may need to unfold.

Today, ask yourself: What thoughts, feelings, needs and desires belong to me, and what belong to others? What is my responsibility, and what is not? How do I stand in my true power?

Brahmacharya : Restraint

The Sanskrit word *brahmacharya* is composed of two words: *brahma* (God) and *charya* (to move with, or follow). It calls us into service to a higher power. Through the history of yoga this calling has emphasized austerity and asceticism, invoking images of emaciated yogis sitting on beds of nails and in faraway mountain caves. Sacrifice, self-discipline and self-restraint continue to be important practices to harness latent spiritual powers and find God. They take us on sacred ground. But we don't have to starve ourselves or leave our loved ones to follow God. Getting up at five a.m. to meditate, meeting personal challenges open-heartedly, or approaching labor with a devotional mindset are worthy sacrifices for any mother or father.

Brahmacharya reminds us to hold our work as parents in sacred regard. It gives our sacrifices purpose and direction, and grounds us in knowing that we don't have to do this work alone.

Today, ask yourself: How can I move closer to my understanding of God in this moment? What can I let go of? How and where can I apply discipline and self-restraint? Where is my sacred ground?

Aparigraha : Non-grasping

Aparigraha is the ultimate practice for mothers. It challenges us to do the impossible: to not hold on to anything, to give up control, and to let life (and birth) unfold as it does. This includes our children. Not holding on to them and letting them become who they are is a perplexing task for mothers. After all, they came from our body: eye lashes, belly buttons, heart chambers and all. They are us.

In the first few months of my children's lives I experienced, like many new mothers, an enduring sense of oneness. It was difficult to tell who was me and who was my baby. With the constant caring and tending that followed over the years these lines remained blurry. My children belonged to me, and I belonged to my children.

But here is the catch: it doesn't work that way. My children don't belong to anyone but themselves. "They are the sons and daughters of Life's longing for itself," Khalil Gibran reminds us. They have their own path in life, including their own timing and pace of growing. This path began long before they were born. Aparigraha urges us to embrace our baby's timing and let go of our ideas on how labor is supposed to go. As contractions come, we don't hold onto them nor do we push them away.

Today, ask yourself: Where am I grasping? Where am I holding my breath, or trying to hard? When do I need to remember to exhale?

Saucha : Purity

Saucha refers to the practice of purity and spaciousness. We strive to keep our living spaces healthy, clean, and in good order. This includes all of our dwelling places: our home, work space, neighborhood, body and mind. We keep things tidy and free of clutter, and our body well-nourished with healthy food, exercise and adequate rest. We aspire to keep our mind pure and simple. Regular housecleaning will help with that. Every day look at your acquisitions, whether they are things or thoughts. Discard what doesn't serve you or makes you sick. Decongest. When we remove excess from our diets, closets, counter tops, schedules and vocabularies we bring more clarity into our lives. Like polishing a window that has not been cleaned in a long time, it lets the sun into our house.

As the mother of three children and wife to a genius but not particularly orderly husband my relationship with saucha has been trying. Keeping your house clean may not be a big deal if you don't have children yet. It certainly wasn't for me before I had children. My home was dusted and organized, and everything was in its place. I get the same impression every time I meet for a private session in the home of a pregnant couple who doesn't have children. The coffee tables are empty, and there are coasters for my water glass. The homes of parents with children are a different story.

Children leave their footprints in our homes, and little feet can make a lot of footprints in one day! Saucha requires parents to do a little rethinking. What does purity mean amidst piles of unfolded laundry and a sink full of dishes? Do dust bunnies and yesterday's breakfast crumbs under the high chair make it a lost cause?

Today, ask yourself: What does purity in my home mean to me? Am I making healthy choices for my body and mind? How can I simplify thinking about labor?

Santosha : Contentment

Santosha is the practice of contentment. It is not a passive experience or the feeling we may have when we get what we want (or sit calmly on a soft meditation cushion). Santosha is about finding contentment when sitting on a bed of nails. It stretches us to accept unwanted and uncomfortable situations, and to attain, amidst them, calmness and peace. Mindfulness and gratitude are two practices I have found to be helpful with this.

Mindfulness calls us to pay attention to what is happening in the moment. Initially we may feel the intensity of whatever nails we are sitting on (a strong emotion, labor pain etc). But if we continue to stay non-judgmentally present, we start to notice other aspects of our experience, and the grip on what's causing us discomfort slowly loosens.

In our first birth class, couples hold ice to practice mindfulness skills. We begin with a "free style" round where parents are asked to notice whatever sensations, thoughts or feelings come up. They often report that holding the ice becomes less painful when they stay curious about what is happening in each moment.

Research in mindfulness-based stress reduction confirms this observation. Pain decreases when we stay with a sensation without reacting to it. Mindfulness neutralizes reactivity and makes room for growth and mature contentment. This is not the same cozy, well-fed contentment as having our needs met. Rather, santosha mirrors the fulfillment of a deeper desire and the inner freedom that comes with it: the freedom of welcoming challenges with a grateful heart.

Today, ask yourself: Am I content in this moment? If not, what is in the way? What can I be grateful for?

Tapas : Discipline

Tapas keeps us on our yoga toes. It is the fire that keeps our practice going, whether this entails daily meditation, a weekly yoga class, an ongoing effort to speak kindly, or remembering to breathe when we feel tense. Tapas doesn't mean you have to lock yourself into a schedule. For me, the fire of tapas is ablaze with two hours of asana practice on some days, and a quiet flame of self-reflection on others. It is okay to be spacious and adjust your practice to your daily capacity and needs. Fire needs air to burn.

But it also needs fuel. Tapas doesn't sit well on comfy couches, it prefers the bed of nails. As the mother of commitment, tapas dares us out of our comfort zone and stretches us into new dimensions. Labor and birth are a perfect arena for tapas. It requires disciplined focus to come back to your breath, to reaffirm trust in the birth process, to gather strength for the next contraction, to not give up.

Today, ask yourself: What practices can I realistically commit to? What areas in my life could benefit from greater discipline? What feeds my fire?

Svadhyaya : Self-study

Svadhyaya is one of my favorite practices and central to the birth classes we teach. It urges us to ponder, honestly, what is real and true about ourselves. This is not always pleasant. Svadhyaya exposes the layers of half-truths and self-deceptions we often use to cover our nakedness. This nakedness scares us because the moment we look we see our imperfections. We see anxiousness, boredom, judgment or greed. No wonder we want to keep this from plain view.

Svadhyaya blows our cover stories and tells it the way it is. Birth does the same. She does not do well with secrets and will leave no stone unturned. When I went into labor the first time, I thought a great deal of myself. But Birth wouldn't have any of it and exposed the secrets I had up my sleeves. Smart?

Gone. Strong? Gone. Special? Gone. I was left utterly naked. Birth wanted me, and she took all she could get.

One of the most challenging things about birth is that you have to go through it yourself. No one will take your place when labor starts. Blindfolded, barehanded, and with a timing that is not of your choosing, you have to cross a stormy ocean. You have to move in ways you haven't moved before, and step into depths you didn't fathom. Your partner and friends can call out to you and keep in touch from the lighthouse of their love, but where you are going no one can follow. It is your solitary path to walk. There are no road maps, cancellations or second chances, and there is nothing you can bring along - except yourself. How you let go. How you hold on. How you face fear. How you forgive. How you love.

When you are in the middle of this ocean, you will meet yourself. It is a guileless encounter, and you will see yourself in your nakedness and innocence. Can you accept, and love, who you may meet? Can you see yourself like a newborn babe? Birth is not a time to bemoan your cries. Hear your cries, yes, and all they speak of —desires, fears and sorrows— and kindly smile upon them. Give them to the ocean, all. With nothing left to let go off, you become the ocean, and there is nothing left to cross.

Today, ask yourself: Who am I? Who do I think I am? Where are my blind spots? How do I face fear? How do I forgive? How do I love?

Isvara pranidhana : Devotion and Surrender

Like the rungs on a spiritual ladder, the yamas and niyamas lead to this final one: devotion and surrender. Isvara pranidhana lifts your personal efforts into the ranks of service and reminds you that your life is a gift to be shared with others. As a pregnant woman, this probably makes sense to you. You share your body with your baby and her growing needs. You forsake sleeping through the night, drinking alcohol, running, laying on your belly. The list of surrenders goes on, and will grow, for years to come, after your baby is born. Isvara pranidhana calls your attention to this noble work as you feel your baby move inside your belly, get up in the middle of the night to use the bathroom, surrender to the task of opening in labor.

But devoting ourselves to our children has limits. As mothers, we get burned out. It is hard to serve another human being day in and out, even if it's cute. It is harder still when the same human being starts talking back and is not interested in what you have to say. I am not the first mother who has asked herself: Why am I doing this? Again?

Isvara pranidhana stretches us to embrace a dignified answer: Above all and everyone, our work is to serve Isvara, God. This is a tall order, and I admit, I am not always good at it. I often prefer having things my way. Often, I get away with it, but frequently I don't. I lock my keys in the car, my kids don't do as I say, or some other annoying thing happens that gets me, well, annoyed. But while I may not like those moments, they are golden. If I remember, in that moment, to let go of my personal drama and ask what God wants me to do, I move with greater strides. She who aims from the mountain top reaches farther than she who aims among trees.

Today, ask yourself: How can I be close to God? How can I serve? What special purpose is uniquely mine?

MOURNING

Birth is a beginning. A new child will be born and a family will grow. Life will be filled with experiences you've never had before, of new places to visit, new words to say, new love to give and receive. But birth is also an ending. It will end your pregnancy and the nine month incubation of dreams and promises. It will end much of the life you had before. In its place, Birth will propose a naked, three dimensional reality, blowing off the sugar dust of your pre-birth fantasies and leaving you with the raw material of Life itself. Maybe it will be sweet. I hope so. But maybe it won't. Labor can be grueling. Things can change in mid-sentence. You had hoped to go without medical interventions but start throwing up in early labor and had to be given an IV. You may have hoped for a beautiful home birth, and end up being transported to the hospital for an emergency Cesarean. Or all goes smoothly with your baby's birth, but weeks down the road you look at your baby with rage and resentment, or don't look at him at all. The end of pregnancy too can be a mixed bag. You may be excited for labor to begin, and are simultaneously filled with trembling confusion. Impatient and ready one day, hesitant and sorrowful the next, you are in the throes of a major transition, without so much as a single contraction!

In our culture, we don't expect women on the verge of birth to feel ambivalent or bewildered. We expect them to be joyful, radiant and eager to meet their baby, and often we shower them with gifts and blessings. We like to celebrate the beginnings – and forget to mourn the endings. Mourning what you are leaving behind does not have to be a sad affair, though many women are quiet weepy as they are nearing full term. Mourning can be as simple as lighting a candle in the spirit of letting go: letting go of having your baby safely tucked in your womb, of having two free hands to use, of sleeping through the night (minus the bathroom break), of not knowing what your life will be like... tomorrow?

When I was in my last trimester pregnant with my third baby, I taught a yoga workshop for mothers in their final month of pregnancy. It was called The Ninth Moon and acknowledged this tender time of pre-labor uncertainty with poetry, story telling and restorative yoga. There are many other ways to celebrate the ending of your pregnancy. You can borrow from the Native American blessing way tradition and gather close female friends to share your joys and sorrows with simple rituals: receiving a foot bath, doing a belly cast, sharing food. Or you can write your endings on strips of paper, burn them and scatter the ashes into a river. You can write a letter to your older self and tell her about all the things you are saying good-bye to now. Whatever you choose, give yourself time to mourn. The following prayer from the Native American Ute nation honors the earth and our capacity for mourning. I always read it to the couples during a meditation in our last class.

Earth teach me stillness as the grasses are stilled with light.
Earth teach me suffering as old stones suffer with memory.
Earth teach me humility as blossoms are humble with beginning.
Earth teach me caring as the mother who secures her young.
Earth teach me courage as the tree which stands alone.
Earth teach me limitation as the ant which crawls on the ground.
Earth teach me freedom as the eagle which soars in the sky.
Earth teach me resignation as the leaves which die in the fall.
Earth teach me regeneration as the seed which rises in spring.
Earth teach me to forget myself as melted snow forgets its life.
Earth teach me kindness as dry fields weep with rain.

I love this prayer and never tire of reading it. It lifts my eyes to the trees and grasses, reminding me that I too am a child of the earth, passing through like melted snow. In mourning of what is no longer, I bow to the beauty in each seed and blade. Mourning the end of your pregnancy prepares you for the beauty of Birth. Her's is a wild beauty that does not fancy standard or style. Birth will make you forget what is up and what is down. She will ask you to let go into a swirling galaxy of possibilities, leaving you at the threshold of a great unknown.

NOT KNOWING

Most pregnant woman fantasize a great deal about the birth of their baby and want to know as much about it as possible. Wanting to know is a normal human desire and part of a necessary awareness shift that helps women get ready to become mothers. Our human need to know prompts us to ask questions, search and research, and connect with others to shed light into our future. Knowledge can be comforting and reassuring as it can enable us to make better choices for ourselves.

Sometimes, however, our quest for knowledge leads us nowhere. The future is a slippery thing: like a bar of wet soap it escapes our grasp when we try to take a firm hold on it. No matter how much time or money we spend in our attempt to know it, we are left where we started: at the feet of a mystery. All you get is a big yawning *No*. You come to realize that you simply can't know. You don't know when labor will start, you don't know how long it will last, you don't know what your baby's birth (or your baby) will be like. This can leave you unraveling. The need to know, fueled by the mind's ceaseless crusade for answers, can become a tense and relentless challenge to handle.

Needing to know is a lot of work. There is value in doing this work but when we start going in circles, it is time to let go and consider the gift of *not* knowing. When I was nine months pregnant with my first baby and the due date arrived, I was equally excited and anxious. As the due date passed by one day, two days, three days, four ... my excitement shifted to fretful apprehension. I couldn't get my mind off the fact that I was now "overdue", and a labor induction was on the horizon. So much for my hope to have a natural childbirth. I tried acupressure, homeopathy, spicy food, sex, and bouncy workouts on the Stairmaster to initiate labor – to no avail. As yet another day went by I became more tightly wound and I would have given anything to know how much longer I'd have to wait. But there was no such answer, and all I could do was wait. Slowly stretched the tongue of time.

If you get past your due date and feel anxious, it can be helpful to put your restless energy into making something with your hands. I started to make a baby mobile for my unborn son. Each day I cut out another piece of felt to make a bird, a frog, a fish and other animals, stuffed it with wool and embroidered it with beads and colored floss. While I was working, time stopped. There was no future to fret about. I got lost in the matching of colors and seams, the steady march of the needle, the quiet heartbeat of my home. While I wasn't any closer to knowing when labor would start, I remembered what I *did* know. I knew I was very pregnant with a boy, it was early spring, and I was making another animal for a baby mobile. There was more, but that was enough. I did not need to know if today was *The Day*, whether I would get induced or have a natural labor. It was okay to not know any of this. That doesn't mean that I wasn't thinking about it. I did. But my thoughts about labor dissolved in the task at hand. There was nothing I could do about the future, but the present was within reach and full of possibilities. It was refreshing, and my anxiety ceased. There was so much to do and to be grateful for, so much to cherish. Why worry about a future that may or may not be?

Around day ten a friend of mine suggested I schedule a massage, and I did. I had completed eight animals and moved on to making a moon and a sun. I worked, and looked forward to my massage appointment the next day. Maybe I would make it, maybe not. It didn't matter. I was comfortable not knowing. I had woven myself into the grain of time, breathing, creating and bowing to the mystery I was part of.

That night, I went into labor. Whether labor started because I was finally at ease, I do not know. I like to believe it did. Many times since then have I noticed that life flows more easily when I've surrendered the need to know and control the next moment, the next hour.

Labor, birth and new motherhood give us plenty of opportunities for relinquishing this need – and for receiving unexpected gifts instead. My need to know (and control) when my baby was sleeping through the night set me off on regrettable sleep training attempts that left me and my baby, in different rooms, choking with tears. My impatience to see my baby sit up, start walking, be out of diapers, finish teething left me reaching for a time that wasn't – and missing out on the time that was. Rushing on, I was deaf and blind to the gifts of those days.

Birthing and parenting are not easy; their gifts are often buried in time. But if we can let go of the future and turn to the present, we gain something no quest for knowledge can match. We remember that life has so much to offer, right here, right now. One of my yoga teachers calls yoga a practice of remembrance. When we slow down, breathe, and tune into the present, we can walk with lighter step. We grow young.

Not knowing is at the heart of mindfulness, or what Zen Buddhism calls *beginner's mind*. Beginner's mind means that you approach each moment with curiosity, openness and enthusiasm. Life is full of wonders! Young children get this. To them, everything is fascinating and worthy of their attention. Not so when we get older. We often forget how to take comfort (and joy) in not knowing. Knowing becomes the thing we pursue and demand. Smart phones, the internet and other sources of information reinforce our belief that everything is knowable. We just have to have the right tools and do the right searches, and the future will be ours. I frequently succumb to this belief. I love having instant access to information. I make use of it frequently, especially when I want to know the outcome of a situation that leaves me anxious and bewildered. It requires some effort to unplug and approach life with beginner's mind. Here is what I do when my need to know gets the better of me: take a deep breath, meditate, take interest in my thoughts and feelings, say affirmations, go outside, make something with my hands, marvel at how difficult it sometimes is to let go (is this the Buddha laughing?), remind myself about the big picture, do what I can do right now. Yes, the dishes will do. In labor, do what you can in the moment. Breathe, move, stay curious. Be mindful.

Breathe – with your whole body
Expand – your mind, your vision, your physical boundaries
Marvel – at the power of your body and the miracle of birth
Inquire – about this moment, your intention
Notice – what's here right now; sight, sound, smell, taste, touch
Detach – yourself from plans, expectations, fear, the next hour
Follow – your body's sensations
Unfold – moment to moment
Love – yourself and your amazing work

TIME-OUTS

A wonderful opportunity to practice mindfulness is when you are resting. Mindfulness itself engenders rest. We can't be mindful and frantic at the same time. The moment we become aware of being frantic or restless, we are not the same person anymore. Our brain has shifted into lower gears. It is cruising at slower speed. Instead of going a hundred miles an hour, we are traveling at sixty, thirty, ten… We start to see our hands on the wheel and can actually read the signs by the road. We may even decide to pull over and spread out, face up, on the grass. Hey, why not? Spontaneous time-outs for rest are powerful equalizers for brains taxed with stress or pain or overstimulation.

When people in our classes talk about how their bodies are feeling I hear a lot of variations of "tired". And this is not only the pregnant moms talking. Everyone is tired. Considering our fast-paced, competitive culture, this is not a surprise. We don't rest enough, we don't move slow. It takes effort to change our speed of living.

When I was pregnant I loved the idea of resting. (I still do.) But more often than not the thought remained just a thought, tucked away in the nebula of my mind for future reference. Inevitably though, I would get so tired that the only way to make it through the rest of the day was to apply restorative first aid. I crawled somewhere under covers and curled up in a ball. When I had enough energy, I would use pillows and blankets to set myself up in a restorative yoga pose. Once situated and comfortable I was always glad I'd made the time for rest and vowed to rest more often. Making time and surrendering to my body's need for downtime was the hardest part. (It still is.) I know this is a challenge for many mothers. Schedules, professional obligations, older children, house work, pets and other personal desires constantly compete for our time and attention. They all want a part of us and our bodies' reserves. Add pregnancy to the mix, and now you have to take a baby into account. As you know, this is not a small thing.

Every day, plan for a bit of rest. When you lay out your day in the morning (or the night before), look for a couple of periods where you can rest. Try to make at least one of them happen. Give yourself a window of fifteen or twenty minutes so that you get in at least ten or more. (If you are like me, you might end up cheating on the time you put aside for rest and steal a few minutes on either end to squeeze in another email, house chore or whatever. Generous planning ahead of time will make it more likely that you get at least some rest.)

To get the most out of your resting time, find a quiet and undisturbed place in your home. You can lie down on a comfortable surface (your bed, a couch, the carpet) or sit down somewhere. You can elevate your legs on chair or on a wall. You can retreat into the bathroom, sit on the toilet or run a bath. If the weather is nice, you can go outside and sit or lie down in the sunshine. If you work out of the home, look for a quiet space in or near your office. Stash a couple of pillows under your desk to maximize your comfort.

Once you have settled your body in restorative time-out, one task remains. For deep rest, you need to draw the curtains of the mind and enter fully into your body. After all, your body is what brought you here in the first place. I like to think of this time as a date with my body, initiated by a wise authority that monitors my level of wellness and balance well beyond what I am capable of. Who am I to argue with it?

So I resign and settle into my body. I feel the tiredness in my bones, and wish I wouldn't be so tired. Wouldn't it be so much nicer to be up and getting things done? I catch myself thinking, and let go of thinking. Start over. Take a breath. Settle in. My body feels tired, heavy, earth-bound. I accept. Yield to the hypnotic pull of fatigue. Notice a slowing in cellular pulsation, like the calming of ocean waves after a storm. Clouds part. Thoughts space out in trailing decrescendo. All motion ceases. All that remains is my breath, silently suspended in mid-day quiescence.

To rest deeply in labor, look for your body's need to rest. You may feel this need as a tension in your shoulders or jaw, or a heaviness in your feet and legs. Your body will be working very hard when it is birthing your baby, so there is no doubt that it will need to rest. It may be easiest to notice your need for rest in between contractions when your uterus is taking a break from the force of labor. Many women actually take mini naps during those breaks. But to enjoy this rest you don't have to wait for the end of a contraction. All of labor is an invitation to rest. Rest is a state of suspension. Motion, effort and engagement ceases. The only movement maintained is connected to the process of breathing and other involuntary functions of the body. Mental activities such as thinking, judgment or worry are suspended. Rest is a sabbatical from it all.

Release
Efface
Submerge
Transform

THOUGHT LABELING

Taking this sabbatical of rest is often easier said than done. Wouldn't it be lovely if our mind would become as motionless as our body the moment we lay down? But often the opposite happens: it goes into overdrive. Our thoughts rev up like race car drivers their engines. And soon we go round and round and round … and then our rest time is up. Our thoughts need some coralling.

Labeling your thoughts for what they are is a helpful strategy for this. Every time you catch your mind wandering during meditation or while resting, you can say to yourself "thinking" or "thoughts". You can even say it out loud, and repeat as often as you wish. When I was a child, I would often say a random word to myself, over and over. I would listen to the word coming out of my mouth, and after a short while it was nothing but sound, morphed into a string of syllables devoid of meaning. Labeling thoughts can have a similar effect. It takes the spine out of our thoughts and eases their grip on our experience.

In one of our birth classes we show a video of a mother who starts out labor with a posterior baby. At some point during labor she is very distraught and starts to cry. She believes her baby will not turn and is afraid that her labor will continue to be painful and difficult. We use this video as an example to discuss assumptions and how our thoughts affect our experience. The thought "my baby will not turn" had a powerful effect on this mother. It filled her with fear and apprehension. If she had looked at this thought with detached interest (labeled it as a mere thought), maybe her labor would have been easier. This is not to say that her anguish and fear weren't important and even necessary aspects of her labor. As it turns out, her baby did turn, and the fact that she acknowledged this thought as fear may have made the difference in her labor outcome.

Thought labeling has, like all practices, their limitations. Some of our thoughts are so compelling that we can't dismiss them as a plain fluctuation of consciousness. This is especially true for experiences that affect our sense of safety, just as it did for this mother. Mind follows such experience like a game dog the call of a hunter's horn. It will run off in search of its prey until it finds what it is looking for. Thought labeling in this case is ineffective. We have to dive into our thoughts and take them at face value. Examining them can help us retrieve coping skills and resources we didn't know we had to support our well-being. The following meditation instruction captures the scope and limitations of thought labeling beautifully:

1. Do one thing at a time.
2. Pay attention to what you are doing.
3. When your mind wanders to something else, bring it back.
4. Repeat step number three a few hundred thousand times.
5. But, if your mind keeps wandering to the same thing over and over, stop for a minute; maybe it is trying to tell you something important.

LOSING IT

As you may remember from my story about Saskia's birth (Birth is Wild), I was afraid to poop into the water. I also didn't want to poop in front of other people. I wanted to keep at least some of my decency (having already stripped off my clothes and composure). I wanted to hold onto some form of control. Birth had touched my Achilles heel and brought me to the final frontier: my ego. This I didn't want to lose.

Losing the ego frightens us. It goes straight to our core and summons existential fears. We are afraid of what may be left of us, afraid to be reduced to nothing. Growing up, we have built our life around ego. Developmentally necessary, ego has helped us make choices and function in the world. It got us through school, and it got us lovers. Ego was there when you decided where to give birth, and when you picked out this book. It certainly was there when I wrote it.

Ego helps us to make sense of the world and helps us to find our place and purpose in it. It motivates and inspires us, and gives voice to identity and character: I am a mother, a teacher, and a writer. I like honey in my tea and 72% dark chocolate. Our ego is a truly wonderful thing! Powerful genie and fulfiller of wishes, it is always at our service. We rub the genie lamp of our desires, and ego appears.

Now, there is nothing wrong with this rubbing. We need our ego to make it through life. But if we don't harness its powers and let ego have its way whenever it wishes, we are in for trouble.

I have to admit that I am not a great fan of writing birth plans. While this can be an empowering and useful exercise to get clear about your needs and wishes, birth plans can easily flex your ego muscle: This is what I want. This is what I don't want. Lets go and get it. Fanning your personal desires for labor and birth may be playing with the fire. You may get burned.

When I went into labor for the first time, there were a lot of things I wanted (neatly spelled out in my 27 point birth plan). I wanted an easy labor, no pain and no drugs. I wanted to feel powerful and strong. I had so much to lose! And lose I did. Birth had me in the trenches, and she had me good. One by one, she claimed it all: my pride, my naivete, my ambition. Stripping off the cloak of my ego, Birth questioned the very center of my self. When she was done, there was not an ounce left of "me".

In birth, ego has no role except for one: to make room for your baby's birth. Your ego needs to become the proverbial lump of salt that dissolves in the sea, not the bolder that sits on the ocean floor. Self-effacing, it has to let go where it wants to cling, wonder where it wants to define, unite where it wants to separate. It needs to answer to a different master.

So it is often when we raise children. On account of being older (and more mature) than my children, I invoke my ego-genie all the time. As their parental guardian, this is my responsibility. I want them to be safe and grow up to be kind and caring people. But letting my ego play the age card ("My genie is bigger than yours!") is not always an advantage when it comes to parenting. When my two year old (with ego in training) wants to take his boots off to walk through puddles, my ego may not like it and suggest otherwise, but does it need to get its way? What do I know about the importance of walking through puddles with no boots on? Or about the necessity of making mud pies, or climbing trees?

Ego doesn't always know what's best. Certainly not for others and not even for ourselves. This is not a surprise. Ego draws its desires from the narrow perceptional field of our individual preferences and programming and often doesn't see the bigger picture. But Birth does. If necessary, Birth will remind you that no matter how hard you stroke the genie-lamp of your desires, you may not get what you want.

Towards the end of writing this book I lost a file with two weeks' worth of writing. These had been a productive two weeks. After more than five years of working on this book, I was nearing the finish line when the file disappeared and with it, weeks of work (including this chapter). I lost it. I panicked, raged, bargained and cried. I had loved every word of my writing; it was good! But now it was gone. Another cosmic joke, divine intervention, or simply a life lesson in letting go; but there was nothing I could do. That night, I picked up my ten year old daughter from a play date at a friend's house after school. Noticing my dismay, she told me that she had learned, in school that very day, about the Buddhist Eightfold Path and the Four Noble Truths. "People suffer because of their attachment to things," she said. "But you can decide if you want to be sad or not. People have a choice." I couldn't help but chuckle, and bet Buddha had a good laugh too.

So I chose. I picked up my genie lamp and called on my ego to help me get back to work. For in the end, there was only one thing to do: the work itself. I remembered how I went into labor the second and third time around. I had decided, quite matter of fact, that I had work to do. Though I knew this work was important, I didn't think of myself as an important player and focused instead on the work itself: the work of breathing and being in my body. I was not conscious of my self, of others in the room, and even of my baby. There was only the work.

The Bhagavad Gita, an old text on the virtues of yoga, speaks to this. The warrior Arjuna, full of questions and anguish as he is facing battle with his kinsmen, seeks counsel from Lord Krishna. Through the course of the Gita, he is shown the path to wisdom. "Perform your duties established in Yoga, renouncing attachment," Krishna tells him, "and be even-minded in success and failure; evenness of mind is called 'Yoga' ... Your right is to work only and never to the fruit thereof. Do not consider yourself to be the cause of the fruit of action; nor let your attachment be to inaction."[6]

Not expecting anything in return for our actions is a foreign concept to the ego. But it is not an impossible one to learn. Looking for the silver lining in a difficult situation, finding gratitude amidst pain, and enlisting our ego in self-

---

6 *Bhagavadgītā* (Gorakhpur: Gita Press, 2010) 38-39.

less service are rewards in itself. With no demands or expectations, we get to see the world with fresh and wondrous eyes, mind-full of great and miraculous beginnings.

DISCERNMENT

A useful practice to detect (and restrain) your ego's affairs is to explore our assumptions. Assumptions are mental byproducts of dealing with uncertainty; they help us fill in the blanks about unknowable situations. Problem is, our assumptions are frequently untrue. They are untrue because a) we don't have enough information, b) the event has not yet occurred, and c) they are heavily shaded by our personal bias. As such, our assumptions tell us a lot more about ourselves than about the issue in question. They are born of our desire for pleasure and of our fear of pain.

While the process of making assumptions is almost impossible to avoid, we can acknowledge them and examine how they affect our life. We can employ different strategies to deal with the unknown. We can breathe. We can pray. We can go upside down in Downward Dog. We can observe the passing of time and become mindful. Mindfulness is the opposite of assumptions, is about *not* knowing and *not* expecting a certain outcome. We are simply aware of the present as it unfurls and let our *experience* have the first and the last word. We don't get ahead of ourselves.

An exercise from our birth class can support you with this. Below you will find thirteen common assumptions about labor and birth. If you want to do the exercise like the couples in our class, have your partner read the following statements to you one by one (instead of reading them by yourself) and share your thoughts with him or her. Ask yourself: Do I believe this statement to be true or not true?

Be honest and spontaneous in your answers. Notice your reactions, especially clear No's. Since this is an exercise about assumptions, your intellect may dismiss some deeper-seated beliefs because, as you know, in birth, *it all depends*. If this is the case, go back over the list, more slowly this time. Pause after each statement, and listen more closely. Try to assume that this statement is true for you, and share what comes up. Then assume that it is *not* true for you, and share with your partner. If you'd rather do this exercise alone, write your observations and thoughts into a journal.

1. Pushing does not hurt as much as dilating.
2. Bigger babies are harder to deliver.

3. If a woman is very tired, her labor will be difficult.
4. Dilation happens at about 1 cm per hour.
5. Transition is short, but very intense.
6. Once a woman reaches full dilation, she will have her baby soon.
7. Labor is one of the most painful experiences in a woman's life.
8. Once a woman reaches full dilation she will have an urge to push.
9. Giving birth is pleasurable, glorious and enjoyable.
10. If a woman is physically fit, her labor will be easier.
11. Giving birth by Cesarean is traumatizing.
12. Contractions get more and more intense throughout labor.
13. Labor will be easier when a woman practices yoga and meditation.

Each of these statements is the result of an experience that was true for someone, likely hundreds and thousands of women. But for many others, they were not true. One of my favorite "untrue" assumptions is #3: "If a woman is very tired, her labor will be difficult." I was exhausted at the end of my second pregnancy, but my daughter's birth was easy and straightforward. Being tired was a blessing in disguise. It helped me surrender to my body's need for rest and make room for my daughter to be born.

What did you notice about the last assumption: "Labor will be easier when a woman practices yoga and meditation"? Isn't that the point of this book? It is indeed. I do hope your yoga will make your labor easier. It certainly worked for me that way. After my first birth, I had started to practice yoga in earnest, and for the most part my second and third labors were calm and easy. But can I know for sure whether yoga made the difference? Maybe it was my practice; maybe it was Venus aligning with Jupiter. Maybe it was the concealed hand of a different conductor. Regardless, if I had to give birth again, I would do my practice, and practice with diligence and passion. Not because I believe in the promise of an easier birth, but because my practice helps me make it through the day. And because you never know.

RIGHT ATTENTION

Many of the above assumptions are about fear of failure. Failure looms large in our competitive culture, and labor is no exception. Many women, especially if they are trying to have a natural, unmedicated birth, fear they won't live up to the task. As a subjective experience, failure is wrapped up in personal desires, values and beliefs and is tied to our definition of success. For example, if you define success in labor as not having an epidural, getting an epidural could easily be perceived as failure.

No mother wants to feel like she failed. It is disempowering and questions her primary role – which is to take care of her children (and the baby she is giving birth to). There are three arenas in which failure can thrive: fantasy, fatigue and fear.

Fantasy belongs to the arena of wishful thinking. Assumptions, projections and expectations fall into this category. When we entertain fantasies, we are often out of touch with reality and are not seeing clearly. This very condition can cause suffering. I went into my first labor with a full blown case of fantasy. I had fantastic ideas about myself and my capacities in labor (without ever having been through one) and fantastic ideas about what birth was. They didn't hold up for long. Reality is always more powerful than fantasy, as dearly as we may cling to our ideas about what reality is supposed to look like.

To steer clear of fantasy and failure, strive to see clearly. Start with coming into the present. Be open and honest with what you see, hear, feel, and notice about yourself. In Buddhism, this is called Right Mindfulness (or Right Attention). Right Mindfulness is part of the Noble Eightfold Path laid out by the Buddha to help his followers develop insight into the true nature of reality and to end suffering. Right Mindfulness, in Buddha's words, means to live "observing (the activities of) the body, having overcome covetousness and repugnance towards the world (of body); observing feelings, having overcome covetousness and repugnance toward the world (of feelings) ... observing (the activities of) the mind, having overcome covetousness and repugnance towards the world (of mind); observing mental objects, having overcome covetousness and repugnance towards the world (of mental objects)"[7].

This practice can be effectively applied to the other two arenas as well. Fear is stressful and can be debilitating, especially if it is prolonged. Chronic stress is toxic for the nervous system. It consumes energy and resources that are unavailable for other physiological functions. A mother who is fearful in labor will likely not only experience more pain but her labor may be also more complicated. Contractions may become less frequent and effective ("failure to progress"), mom may need pain medication or a Cesarean delivery ("failing" to have a natural birth), or baby may have lower Apgar scores ("failing" her first health test).

Fear feeds on fatigue. A difficult pregnancy, a long labor, or struggling with labor pain can contribute to overwhelming fatigue in labor. No brain functions well when tired. While we may rely, in our day-to-day lives, on stimulants

---

7 Walpola Rahula, *What the Buddha Taught* (New York: Grove Press, 1974) 110.

(caffeine, sugar) to keep going, this may not be a good option in labor. A healthier option here is to get rest and sleep. If you are so tired that your brain is not able to run the "restorative time-out tape", pain medication may give you what your body so desperately needs. The two hour nap I enjoyed after getting an epidural during my first labor gave me enough energy to birth my son vaginally. Resting your mind in reality and mindfully observing what is happening within and around you disables the failure potential of fantasy, fatigue and fear.

BE STILL AND KNOW

Sometimes in labor, while parenting, or just in life in general our mind needs more support and structure than our skill at meditation can offer. The promise of peacefulness eludes us, try as we may. In those situations I spin my prayer wheels. I turn inward and submit a humble petition to the One Source that has many names. One of my favorite prayers is part of a bible psalm: "Be still and know that I am God." Archbishop Desmond Tutu and his daughter Mpho Tutu share a meditation based on this psalm in their book "Made for Goodness"[8]. You begin the meditation with an inhale and say in your mind "Be still and know", and finish with an exhale and say "that I am God". With each following breath you omit one word at the end of the sentence:

Be still and know that I am God
Be still and know that I am
Be still and know that
Be still and know
Be still and
Be still
Be

After several breaths of silence, you can reconstruct the prayer word by word if you like. You can also repeat certain passages several times, or space out the phrases. I use this prayer meditation frequently when sleep escapes me at night. Within moments, it grounds me, my breath takes over, and I enter into a state of deep rest.

If you have any favorite prayers or mantras, bring them into labor, maybe on a nice card you've decorated, and use them as you wish. Birth is a sacred event. In Buddhism and Hinduism, the birth of a child signals the beginning of

---

8 Desmond Tutu and Mpho Tutu, *Made for Goodness* (New York: Harper Collins, 2011).

a new cycle of *samsara*, the turning wheel of birth, life and death which resumes the unfolding of one's karmic path. Each birth is understood as a rebirth and another opportunity for the reincarnated being to shed karmic debt accumulated in past lifetimes as a result of unskillful actions. Being born a human and endowed with human consciousness is an auspicious, blessed event. Only humans have the capacity to understand the true nature of reality and to be liberated from the cycle of samsara. New Hindu and Buddhist parents have a big repertoire of rituals to celebrate the opportunity for liberation that is given to the soul joining their family.

Parents in the U.S. have fewer, if any, birth rituals that honor the sacredness of childbirth. But with research, preparation and intention, you can find powerful birth blessings for your baby. Try using the above prayer to bring yourself to a place of stillness, and wait for words to come. Maybe they arrive fully articulated and spelled out to a T, maybe they come as a feeling in your body. Be still and know.

ACCEPTING

Acceptance is a core practice in many spiritual traditions. It is often one of the most difficult ones. Acceptance asks us to bow to the circumstances we are presently facing, and surrender to what cannot be changed. Accepting is typically difficult when our desires are incongruent with conditions favorable to the fulfillment of our desires. What we want and what is presently possible are two different things. Our ego is usually challenged by this. It doesn't like it when things don't go the way it wants. Instead, it bargains, lobbies, argues, wails and insists. But when it runs out of options, acceptance becomes a possibility.

One morning I was driving home after dropping my youngest daughter off at school. It was a particularly rainy morning in early fall after a weekend of strong winds, and I figured there would be traffic. I tried to calculate which road would be the best to take home (i.e. the least jammed up with traffic) and which park to go to as I had my dog in the car and she still needed to get exercise. However, my choice of road turned out as good as any: there was traffic. I took the next exit, hoping I would beat it, but other drivers must have had similar thoughts. To make matters worse, the traffic was backed up due to road construction, and other roads were closed. Now I didn't even have the option to go another way. I was stuck. I felt myself bristling and cursing my choices. Now I would be home a lot later than I wanted and had less time to do what I wanted. While I was sitting there in traffic, my mind started going a hundred miles an hour, looking for others to blame, seething with impatience and frustration.

But then something shifted. Whether the shift started in my ears as they heard rain pounding on the car roof, or in my eyes as they caught a watery reflection of lights in the street, I do not know. I felt like waking up from a trance. The mental nightmare of chasing after my desire to be some place where I was not was gone. It didn't matter what time it was or where I was. I felt simply alive. My mind quickly took interest. How soothing was the sound of the rain. How quiet the breath and the wind in the trees.

I drove home unhurriedly, and stopped on the way to play ball with my dog at the park. Freed from wanting what was not, I was able to enjoy what was. The wet grass, the rain washed air, my dog with her silly antics.

Because our desires are so powerful, they can demand a great deal of time and attention. They are a hungry litter, but neither can nor should we always feed them. Feeding into my desire to be somewhere else that morning in the car was neither useful nor pleasant. Investing mental assets into what I didn't have (and what wasn't) spoiled my morning. Letting go of my desire and turning toward what I had (and what was), returned the morning back to me, in its perfect assembly, and with an unexpected gift besides. It made room for the fulfillment of a deeper desire: my soul's desire for joy and happiness. It is a winged desire. It can only alight when we attend to what is.

When we allow ourselves to be drawn into the present and become willing dwellers of the Here and Now, we are well on our way to acceptance. This includes our willingness to attend to the hard parts. Being present with what is can be painful, agonizing, confusing, meaningless, even when the sun is shining and the sky is blue. The secret to acceptance is to notice and to accept it all: the pain, the confusion, and the blue sky (which is sometimes the most difficult to accept).

A helpful practice for deepening acceptance is to write down everything that is hard for you to accept in the present moment. I call it the Creed of Acceptance. Start each sentence with "I accept". Keep writing until you can't think of anything else to accept. If you are in labor, you can say those thoughts out loud. If I would have written a Creed of Acceptance during my first labor, it would have looked like this:

I accept that I am in pain.
I accept that this pain is hard to bear.
I accept that I don't know what to do.
I accept that it is the middle of the night.
I accept that the birth ball is purple.

I accept that my husband and doula are trying to help me.

I accept that I don't believe they can help me.

I accept that I am scared.

I accept that the fetal monitor is tight around my belly.

I accept that I am in labor.

I accept that this is harder than I thought.

I accept that I was wrong about labor.

I accept.

Mind and ego tend to fixate on one particular aspect of an experience. Soon, this aspect becomes our all-consuming reality, and we are trapped, like I was trapped in traffic that morning. But when we attend to other aspects of an experience, we start to release our mind's monopoly on reality and can begin to see what is true and receive the gifts therein. With acceptance, the day of your baby's birth, however it may unfold, will not become Judgment Day. It will be a Thanksgiving.

ON THE MAT

Regular, formal practice, whether on the mat or a meditation cushion, may not be right for you. For me, it is mandatory. It keeps my body and brain healthy, combats complacency and inertia, and keeps me focused on the path. This is not always fun, especially at six in the morning when my alarm goes off to remind me that it's time to get up if I want to have time to practice before work.

I may bargain with dawn to give me a few more minutes in bed. It is warm and the place my body wants to be. But then I remember and peel my bones out from under the covers. Desire moves my feet and rolls my yoga mat out on the studio floor where I practice an hour later.

Desire is an old, familiar friend. It led me to my first yoga class because I wanted to have an easy birth. Years later, it got me out of the house looking for a break from my children, for a hardwood floor without dust bunnies and scattered toys, for silence. I wanted to touch my toes in a forward bend, sit in Lotus pose, know what it was like to live in a body that can balance in a handstand. Desire kept me going, and I am glad it did. Not because it got me some of the things I had wanted, but because it got me something better. Like the heroine in a fairy tale, I went on a journey with my mind set on returning with what I set out to find, but returned with something else instead. I found myself. But it's not a glamorous attainment. I do not return to the sound of drum rolls and with flying banners. My homecoming is a quiet one.

One of my first yoga teachers compared the yoga mat to a mini-cosmos of our lives. Every time we practice, we zoom into ourselves and our habits, or into what Mark Epstein calls "powerful reactions [that] have the capacity to take hold of us and drive our behavior"[9]. In yoga and Buddhism, these powerful reactions are called *kleshas*. Like shackles, they limit our range of motion, but in a rather mental, phenomenological way. They confine us to a pre-ordained place of existence and dictate how we see the world. There are five kleshas: ignorance (avidya), ego (asmita), attachment (raga), aversion (dvesa) and fear of death (abhinivesah). Avidya, or ignorance, is at the root of those five. Ignorance here doesn't mean lack of intelligence or education, but refers to our ineptness in realizing our true nature. Adi Shankara, a great mystic saint who lived in India two thousand years ago, describes this nature in his Song of the Soul: "Neither knowable, knowledge nor knower am I, formless is my form. I dwell within the senses but they are not my home. Ever serenely balanced, I am neither free nor bound. Consciousness and joy am I, and Bliss is where I am found."

We all have this beautiful, bliss-filled soul, are angels with wings, but are often blind to it. Our fascination with the temporary and transient and our need for control keep us distracted from knowing our light. How often have I vowed to myself to make more time for meditating, to pace myself, to breathe more, to look up to the sky, and have cleaned the house or given orders instead, letting my ego have the last word.

Asmita, our ego, and its identification with the body and mind reinforces avidya (ignorance). We believe that we are our body, and often believe the stories our mind tells us about who we are. This is the ego's finest accomplishment, and it defends it fiercely. We are attached to the things ego procures: name, identity, status, relationships, health, illness. Sri Nisragadatta, one of the greatest contemporary sages of India, reminds us that it is attachment to "a name and shape that breeds fear", including our fear of death (abhinivesah). "Consistently and perseveringly separate," he urges, "the 'I am' from 'this' or 'that' and try to feel what it means to be, just to be, without being 'this' or 'that.'"[10]

Usually "this" or "that" wait for me on my mat when I start to practice. They wait for me as raga (attachment) and dvesa (aversion), and always come hand in hand. As ego's kin, they reach for my toes and pine for my nose on my shin. They steal peeks to the woman next to me who is practicing a full and seemingly effortless split. But when it is my turn to do the pose, I resist. My hips and hamstrings are burning, and I don't want to feel this. I am afraid of the

9   Mark Epstein, *Going on Being* (New York: Broadway Books, 2002), 126.
10 Sri Nisargadatta Maharaj. *I Am That* (Durham: The Acorn Press, 2012), 54.

pain, and afraid to get hurt. I hold back and try to remember to breathe. Be here. Be with this and that. Be with it all, with my ignorance, my pain, my fears and desires. Be with my struggling, beautiful self.

Sometimes, and effortlessly, an understanding emerges from this: the realization that I am neither. I am neither this nor that. This is the gift of practice. It offers me glimpses, ephemeral and ever beckoning, into my soul. It is quiet there and serene, a benevolent place of homecoming. I am.

Inevitably, the moment fades, and I'm back in the this or that. I go through the motions, looking for the DNA of yoga, the hidden fibers in a stretch.

In Hinduism, a religion rich with colorful stories of supreme beings, this essence is called amrit. It is the heavenly nectar of immortality, retrieved by the gods at the beginning of time. In the Hindu story of churning the cosmic ocean, gods and demigods join efforts to churn the Milky Way to bring the universe back into balance. It is a difficult enterprise, and one that almost fails. The mountain used for the churning rod sinks. Deadly poisons are stirred up that almost kill the crew. If it weren't for Lord Vishnu, who secures the mountain, and for Lord Shiva, who swallows the lethal poison, all would be lost. But it is not, and amrit, the elixir of ever-lasting life, is recovered.

The story does not end here, and it does not end after I get off my yoga mat. The taste of sweetness lingers for a while and then it disappears, leaving me with a divine addiction. So I go back again, roll out my mat, and keep churning my cosmic ocean. Like in the story of amrit, I come up, each time, with all kinds of "poisons". Still, I churn away, swallowing pride, greed, jealousy, ego and fear. It is a tiresome labor, but a labor worthwhile. It is a rehearsal for life and all its birthing moments. Regular, formal practice supplies the momentum.

When I was in my third trimester with my last baby, I meditated every night before bed. I would light a candle on a small birth altar I had set up, and gaze at the light for a couple of minutes. Then I would close my eyes and sit for a few minutes longer. I listened to my breath and the day unwinding in my house with bedtime routines and stories. I didn't repeat any mantras or affirmations but just sat quietly, letting any distractions fade into the falling of night. When I went into labor nights later, I picked up my practice where I had left off: noticing, breathing, and letting go as my body turned into a churning ocean.

To poet Sylvia Plath, being a mother is "no more ... than the cloud that distills a mirror to reflect its own slow effacement at the wind's hand." I have not found a more fitting description of what it's like to become a mother. Just like the cervix melts and disappears during labor, the becoming of mother hinges on the slow and often painful fading of what she thought was herself.

Every time I practice on the mat, this becoming and un-becoming continues. It is the reason why I go. I am dying to see where it takes me.

GRATITUDE

The practice of gratitude is one of my favorites. When I am grateful, I am in loving relationship with Creation. I don't feel separate or lost in my dramas but connected to the matrix of all things: the rose I stop to smell, the brow of my daughter's eye, the tears on the face of a stranger or on my own. Gratitude is an unequivocal *yes* that flows directly out of mindful presence, whether the present moment bears joy or pain. But it is not the stoic *yes* of acceptance. Gratitude is a mystical experience and the *Yes!* that soars on the wings of Grace. It is where labor becomes loving, and Love the channel to liberation.

Years ago, I was sick with the flu. After many days in bed, I got up one morning and noticed the plum tree in our back yard. It stood there in full bloom. The tree, though rather old and gnarled, looked like a young girl dancing with the wind, leaving as tokens of affection white petals on the ground around her, giving herself away, lighthearted and smiling. A small sadness welled up within me. I wanted the tree to stay the way it was, in full bloom against the deep blue sky. I didn't want it to shed its pretty blossoms but the tree shook her head and whispered: Silly! Don't you see? There are so many! There is so much to give!

I remembered my daughter Hanna who, when she was preschool age, would often leave bracelets, hair clips, shells or special pebbles with one of her friends. I would see Hanna leave in the morning for school with a handsome assembly of sparkly barrettes in her hair, and pick her up in the afternoon without a single one left. "Oh", she would casually say, "I gave them away." There is so much to give.

But what had I to give now? I had the flu, and felt miserable and weak. Giving seemed to come from a place of strength and abundance – none of which I had at the moment. For days, all I could *do* was let the hot blade of fever fight its dutiful battle, stripping my mind down to reptilian awareness. Gone was my ability to think, make plans, or manage a simple task. Instead, time was measured by vague sensations as I drifted in and out of sleep: The coolness of a washcloth on my forehead, the voices of my children ringing like silver bells, the lava of my breath laboring from my mouth. There were no thoughts, no words, no concepts. I was nobody.

This wasn't easy to accept. I had always taken comfort and pride in being a mother, a wife, a teacher, a friend, but now none of this mattered. The flu, just as Birth before, had left me on the anvil of experience, reducing my identities, cravings and fears to – nothing. There was no before and no after, only the all-consuming Now.

The lure to return to "my" world felt strong at times – such as when my two year old trundled into my room and looked at me with a mix of uncertainty, disappointment and longing. Tears welled up in my eyes, wanting to hold and nurse her, wanting to be mother. Too weak to lift her next to me, she would eventually leave the room to play with her siblings.

My heart was full with the memories of this surrender as I looked at the tree. I saw my children being born and learning to walk; and I saw the flowers of the plum tree ripen into fruit. I saw my children picking fruit into their little blue bucket, the juice of sun-ripened plums running down their faces, and then I saw the leaves falling. I saw the rock at the base of the tree where I had buried the palm-sized body of a baby I miscarried, and I saw the tree come to life again – a symphony of white clusters, amidst its branches the Buddha, sitting and smiling.

He was sitting there, watching the world from within, watching it with its departures and arrivals, struggles and passions. He smiled, and I smiled, suddenly overwhelmed with love. Everything was so absolutely perfect, beautiful, and precious. I felt like I had just given birth, my heart paper thin, vulnerable and untouched like the web of skin between a newborn's fingers. I felt I was seeing the world for the first time – a spectacular place of immeasurable beauty. Maybe I didn't have much to give right then and there, but I could always Give Thanks. And as if in response to my thanksgiving, the wind brushed the plum tree and gathered the miracle of a dozen heart shaped petals into my cupped hands.

Formal Practice

Do your practice, and all is coming.
~ Pattabhi Jois

COMMITMENTS

Henry David Thoreau said that a truly good book compels the reader to "lay it down, and commence living on its hint. What I began by reading, I must finish by acting". I hope I have inspired you to start up a regular yoga practice, deepen an existing one, and above all, commit to it. Let your thoughts upon waking include the desire to practice that day. Bump your formal practice time up on the to-do list. Pause throughout the day to bless the present moment however it meets you. Bless the last thoughts at the end of your day with a thanksgiving for the time you spent practicing.

"See you soon and often," my dear yoga teacher Casey Palmer tells me when I leave his studio at the end of my practice. I love his reminder to practice regularly because it doesn't take much to get pulled back and lost in the dramas of my life. To practice, with diligence and passion, is to transcend the power struggles, uncertainties, and dirty dishes. It keeps the veil of Maya, the illusion that I am separate and distinct from the rest of creation and God, from clouding my vision.

Commitment to practice is an important part of our Yoga Way to Birth classes. Early in the program, we ask couples to decide on a formal practice that works for their lives and interests (such as meditating for ten minutes every day, or taking two yoga classes per week) and to make a commitment to another class participant (randomly chosen and not their intimate partner) to follow through with it. In a later class, everyone is asked to share with their class partner how their practice went, and to renew their commitment to practice. In a second homework assignment I ask couples to sit and meditate, one time, for thirty minutes. When they get back a week later to share about their experience, usually about half the group reported that they completed the assignment. They appreciated the opportunity to sit quietly, the revival of a withered practice, the stretching of their comfort zone. Which half do you choose to be in?

WILLINGNESS

Commitment to regular practice begins with willingness. On a meditation retreat I attended, the teacher described mindfulness as "an intentional application of attention to bring about a shift from willful practice to the practice of willingness". Willful practice follows schedules and structures. I practice willfully when I make a plan to go to yoga and follow through with it. Willfulness also applies when I bring my focus back to the breath as I move from one posture to the next, or when I decide to hold a pose one breath longer.

But willfulness alone can become rigid and lifeless when it lacks curiosity. *Willingness* fosters curiosity, and curiosity doesn't require a schedule. All it takes is the decision to be present, to ask honest questions, admit weaknesses, give up excuses, accept who you are, take responsibility for yourself, and commit to doing it all over. Willingness is about being real. Labor and birth are real, very real. They too require you to be present, to ask honest questions, admit weaknesses, give up excuses, accept who you are, take responsibility for yourself, and commit to doing it all over – with each new contraction.

The practices in this chapter are based on traditional yoga and meditation techniques and meant to be an inspiration for your own practice path. I hope you walk this path with passion and thoughtful urgency. Whatever practice draws you inward, trust it. It's the place to go.

DANCE OF THE BALLOON

Yoga is a meditative practice. Whether you sit still on a meditation cushion, move through a series of poses, chant, or read spiritual texts, you are engaging your mind in a meditative discourse.

The word "meditation" goes back to the Old Latin and French word for study. It draws its meaning from the root med~, which means to measure, limit or consider. This semantic detail is helpful to understand what we do during meditation. We measure, limit, and consider.

One of my yoga teachers compared meditation to the string that holds a helium filled balloon. Without the string, the balloon, or our thoughts, would fly off. Meditation limits the range of our thoughts. It reigns them in. To help with this, we measure out the length of string through various meditation techniques. Those techniques fall into two categories: object and object-less meditation.

Object meditation focuses the mind on a specific object such as the breath, a mantra or an image. It's a good practice for beginners as it keeps the "mind-balloon" on a shorter string. When the mind wanders off, we give a tuck on the "string", so to speak, and bring our focus back to our meditation object. Object-less meditation doesn't use objects. It allows for a longer "string" and lets the mind roam more freely.

Both meditation approaches are helpful in preparation for and during labor. They teach the mind to sustain attention, help us stay present, and facilitate memory training. Meditation invites us to listen to the rhythms of our inner state. We touch the mesh of our cellular landscape with awareness. We look for and recognize patterns.

Recognizing patterns is part of learning. Patterns foster comprehension and meaning. As we make repeated effort to be present, we define and continually redefine where we are in relationship with ourselves and how we are in relationship with what is. It is where we get to watch the dance of the balloon.

PRACTICAL GUIDELINES

There are three ways to practice: formal, informal, and perpetual.

With formal practice, you set a regular time aside for a specific practice routine, let's say every morning between 7 and 7:30am. You can sit and meditate, do a set of breathing exercises, or roll out your yoga mat and practice asana. The point is that you intentionally show up for your practice, ideally around the same time each or most days.

Informal practice occurs throughout the day whenever you remember or notice the need to orient or anchor yourself. You take a time-out from what you are doing and look inward to assess where you are and what you need in the moment. This can be a stretch at the desk, a couple of deep breaths, a prayer, a mantra, a thanksgiving. You can sit quietly in your car before you start the engine, or tune into your body when you prepare food, eat, do the dishes, feel edgy, restless, or excited. There are a thousand ways to practice, and each one counts. Informal practice brings your yoga "home", i.e. into your daily actions and relationships – which is where they matter.

Buddhist teacher DaeJa Napier calls the present moment a portal to access patience, kindness and compassion. Informal practice is your key to this portal and especially beneficial when we need a good dose of patience, kindness, or self compassion. Showing up for yourself in a time of need can turn a difficult situation into a moment of transformation.

This is a bonus of the third way of practice: perpetual. At this stage, practice is our modus operandi. Everything we do is immersed in practice, and practice is immersed in everything we do. This, at least, is what we strive for in every waking moment (and, with advanced practice, in our sleep and dreaming too).

Ideally, both formal and informal practice approaches are part of your birth preparation. Building a disciplined formal practice is often not easy when you are pregnant, and especially as a new mother. My formal personal practice has become more consistent only after my youngest child started school.

Try to start with five minutes of formal practice every other day. You can keep this time unstructured as you begin, and just sit or lie down. Don't worry about figuring out what your practice should look like. Simply make the effort to show up by making time for it. Remember, all of your practice is good practice. You can't go wrong when you practice – even if you feel confused, disappointed with the results, or madly distracted. It is all part of the training. Keep in mind that you are on a path, and trust that your efforts will pay off, whether during labor or at some other point in the future. Be earnest, and persevere. All is coming.

Traditionally, yoga and meditation are practiced in the morning upon first waking. In this way many of the practice benefits (mental calmness, clarity, healthy circulation and metabolism) can carry over into the rest of your day. Before you begin, decide how long you want to practice. The best advice I have heard on how to long to practice comes from Buddhist teacher Yongey Mingyur Rinpoche[11]. He suggests to spend less time meditating (or practicing) than you think you can. If you think you have ten minutes, stop at eight or nine. Keep it shorter on purpose. This way you avoid trying too hard or thinking you accomplished a goal, and you may want to come back for more.

Most practices in this book are suitable for ten minutes or less. More importantly than for how long you are practicing is that you are practicing. If it works better for you to take five minutes several times throughout the day versus twenty minutes in one stretch, then do so. Be realistic in your commitment, but be committed.

It is helpful to have a dedicated space for your practice. This doesn't have to be anything fancy; a small private area in your home where you won't likely be interrupted can suffice. If you are inspired, you can set up a small birth altar. In our Yoga Way to Birth classes, we assemble a birth altar at the beginning of each class. Couples bring one or two meaningful objects to place on this altar. I am always touched by their thoughtful (and sometimes whimsical) choices: a pair of little baby booties, gem stones, small figurines of deities, a stuffed animal. The altar stays arranged until our closing meditation during the last class.

---

11 Yongey Mingyur Rinpoche, *The Joy of Living* (New York: Harmony Books, 2008).

If you can't make mornings work and evening times work better for you, wait until at least one hour after dinner, especially if you plan to include movement. Practicing at the end of the day is a great way to let go of accumulated stress and enter peacefully into the nighttime hours. As labor often starts at the end of the day or during the night, evening is a special time to spend with your body, your breath and your baby. During my third pregnancy, the evening was my preferred time. I left my husband with the dishes and my children, and meditated in the bedroom adjacent to our living room on the sounds of our home unwinding. Some weeks later, this is when my labor started.

Five Sense Meditations

Our five senses –sight, hearing, smell, taste and touch– are readily available meditation tools to use during labor. They don't require any setup and have evolved over thousands of years for the purpose of sensory perception, orientation and momentary awareness. When we focus on one of our senses, we lift our body's experience out of oblivion. We honor its part in the world and bow to its technicolor wisdom.

There are at least two ways to work with our senses during meditation: as is, or intentionally.

No refunds or returns: Practicing as is

Practicing as is hones in on the essence of mindfulness. If you have bought something at a second hand store before you were probably happy with your purchase, even if it wasn't brand new or in perfect shape. Practicing as is captures this experience. You accept (and may even celebrate) what you discover without wishing anything to be different.

For example, let's say you decide to meditate on sound. You sit down, close your eyes, and listen to the sounds around you. You may hear your breath, a clock ticking, cars driving by outside. You may hear your cat scratching at the door. You hear her scratching again. Now she starts meowing. Instead of getting irritated or feeling worried about her, you stay with the sounds as they occur. You can say to yourself: scratching, or sound. Either way, you keep the auditory input as is.

Custom ordered: Practicing intentionally

With intentional practice you imbue a sensory perception with a desired emotional quality. In the above example, you could regard the sound of your cat with love in your heart. You could say to yourself: My cat loves me. I love my cat.

If you wish, you can take this to another level and practice loving kindness, one of four Buddhist mindfulness practices called Brahma Viharas. The first Brahma Vihara, loving kindness or metta, is at the heart of Buddhism: It cultivates friendliness and goodwill toward all sentient beings. Loving kindness is practiced formally by repeating a short verse. There are many variations on this verse, but here is my favorite:

May you be happy.
May you be peaceful.
May you be free from inner and outer harm.
May you be free.

This verse can be applied to yourself, to another person, an animal or other sentient being. Anything you hear (such as your cat meowing or a crying baby) or see (a person struggling with homelessness in the street, your own reflection in the mirror) can be used as a reminder to practice loving kindness. I always end the last Yoga Way to Birth class with this meditation, addressing parents and their unborn babies alike.

Another helpful intentional practice for labor is to meditate on impermanence. Everything in life, without exception, is transient. Day changes into night, clouds to rain, earth to dust. So too do our bodies, thoughts and feelings change. Anything we feel, hear, see, smell or taste gives way to other sensations. Your cat won't meow for ever. Contractions will come and go.

Meditating on Sight

To meditate on sight, choose an object you'd like to focus on. Place it at eye level two to three feet in front of you with your eyes lowered toward the tip of your nose. Elevate the object on a small shelf or bench if needed so that your eyes stay restful but alert. Let your gaze rest on the object. Try not to think about what you see, simply hold the image of your object in quiet awareness. For intentional practice, you can choose an object with a special meaning, for example:

- Roses- for love and beauty
- Rosemary- for devotion and remembrance
- Chamomile- for relaxation

- Bird's feather- for lightness and ease
- Candle- for your heart flame
- Precious rock- for solidity and endurance
- Bamboo- for flexibility

Let your gaze rest upon the object, and breathe quietly and deeply for the duration of practice.

Labor & birth: Any of the above objects can serve as a focus during labor, but anything you are visually resonating with can do the job, whether you choose the object ahead of time or discover it in the moment. One momma I have worked with focused on the pattern of her midwife's socks, so really, anything goes.

Meditating on Sound

Close your eyes (if you can safely do so), and listen to the sounds that naturally surround you — the sound of wind or rainfall, your breath, a clock ticking, phone ringing, your body digesting. Listen to sounds coming in through your right ear and through your left ear. Listen to sounds close up, and sounds far away. Listen to your baby. Can you hear the very beginning of a particular sound, and its ending? Can you hear the silence?

Meditating on Smell

Our sense of smell is one of the oldest sensory systems of the body. One of the most advanced senses babies have at birth, it develops around 11 to 15 weeks of gestation, two full months before sight and hearing come on board. It is the first to introduce us to life on earth after we are born.

For practice and labor support, select scents you like. Are there any smells that invoke happy memories? Experiment with essential oils or flower essences. Hold one at a time to your nostrils and take a couple of regular breaths. Notice whether you like the smell. Do you want more, or rather not? If the scent is pleasant, take a deeper breath. Let it linger. Does it remind you of anything? If you have a positive association with the scent, you can use it during labor. Essential oils blend well in massage oil or diluted in water in a spray bottle. Some olfactory associations you may find amenable:

- Cypress, Grapefruit, Orange- for confidence
- Frankincense, Lemon, Orange, Bergamot- for joy
- Chamomile, Lavender- for relaxation

Labor & birth: In addition to the scents in this list, you can bring a soap or lotion you (and your partner) particularly like, or any scent that reminds you of comfort and home. If you are able to take a walk outside, become aware of the smell of the air, the season, trees, the rain. And if that's possible, remember to bury your nose in the folds of your baby's skin after she is born. There is no other smell like it.

Meditating on Touch

Meditating on touch utilizes the largest sense organ of our body: our skin. Containing different type of nerve endings programmed to identify temperature, pressure, vibration or stretch, our skin literally brings us in touch with our physical surroundings. Here are some general practice ideas:

- Sit back to back with your partner. Notice each other's body and breath.
- Wrap yourself in a special scarf or blanket during meditation. Notice the scarf on your skin. Have the scarf next to you when you are in labor.
- Lay down on grass.
- Throughout the day, notice the temperature of air on your skin.
- Take a bath in clear, unscented warm water.

Labor & birth: As many mothers in labor close their eyes during labor to concentrate on contractions, focusing on touch is a readily available meditation tool for both mothers and birth partners. If your partner has learned massage or acupressure techniques for labor support, you can make the feeling of his or her hands your focus.

Meditating on Taste

For formal practice prior to labor make yourself a cup of raspberry leaf tea and drink it slowly. Set the cup down after each sip, and send a blessing to your uterus. Each meal you eat provides another opportunity to meditate on taste. Take a small portion of food only, set your fork or spoon down after each bite, chew slowly, discover the various flavors, and observe the different processes involved when swallowing and nearing satiation. Concentrate on its unique taste, texture and temperature, on the way it changes, and on any lingering sensations.

Labor & birth: Women in active labor usually don't want to eat, but a small portion of food or sips of juice in between contractions go a long way to keep up energy and as a meditative focus. Experiment with a small mint, a sip of orange juice or honey-sweetened tea. Try ice chips or plain water.

BREATHING PRACTICES

There are many ways to utilize breathing in labor, from relaxed and rhythmic breathing to counting your breath, panting and vocalizing.

All can be useful in labor and lend themselves to various techniques, but my favorite way to work with the breath is through breath awareness.

Breath awareness is an active, curious noticing of each breath as it arises, without trying to change or react to it. This is different from breathing techniques. I believe we don't need to learn so much how to breathe as we need to become aware that we breathe. We need to put the know before the how.

This is not to say that breathing techniques can't be helpful in labor, especially during the pushing phase. In our experience birth helpers (midwives, doulas etc) become more involved in the management of labor at that time and tend to coach the laboring mother directly with suggestions how to breathe. Breath awareness as a cornerstone allows other breathing techniques to be experienced more fully.

To practice breath awareness, notice each breath as it happens. Take gentle interest, letting each breath occur naturally. Pay attention to patterns. What makes the inhale an inhale and the exhale an exhale? Is the breath even, smooth and rhythmic? Additionally, you can notice:

- breath entering and exiting through your nose
- the length of your inhalation and exhalation
- the temperature of air at the nostrils during inhale and exhale
- the movement of your ribcage
- the movement of your diaphragm
- the movement of your belly
- the length of space at the end of inhale and at the end of exhale
- the space between breaths
- the depth of each breath

If your mind is very restless, you can include a mantra, counting or a visualization (see below) to your breath awareness and practice breath awareness within more technical structures.

Welcome Breath

Take a Welcome Breath when you start your meditation or yoga practice, when you need to ground yourself, or at the beginning and end of a labor contraction. Just take a deeper breath than usual, and welcome where you are. It is the exact place to be.

Counting

- Counting the breath is a traditional concentration technique. Take one full breath, and think "one". Take another breath, and think "two". Carry on in the same way until you get to "ten". This completes one set. (Think "first set".) If getting to ten is a reach, use shorter sets.

- Try counting backwards from 27. If you lose track, start over. As you develop the ability to make it all the way to "one" without losing your count, you can practice for four sets total. This makes 108 breaths, an sacred number in yoga and Buddhism with many auspicious meanings.

- Count your breath during labor contractions. The average respiratory rate in a healthy adult at rest is between 12–18 breaths per minute. As you want to aim for deep and restful breathing during labor (and contractions last about one minute), counting to 12 (or 13, if this is your lucky number) may be a good place to start.

- Use counting during the most challenging part of a contraction. With an average active labor contraction lasting about 45 seconds, the most intense part may be about 20 or 30 seconds. Twenty to thirty seconds amounts to about six breaths. Six breaths to ride the crest of the wave. Sounds doable, doesn't it?

Womb Opening Breath

This breath utilizes visualization. Visualizations are powerful mental techniques that can focus the mind and gather momentum toward a desired outcome. For the Womb Opening Breath, begin your inhale in your lower pelvis. Imagine that your inhalation picks up molecules of love and light as it passes through your abdomen, lungs and heart. When you exhale, imagine these molecules flowing over your womb, placenta and baby, permeating and softening your cervix from the inside out.

Breath Mantras

A mantra is a sacred word, syllable or phrase used as an object of concentration. Because of the rhythmic nature of the breath, two-syllable mantras are ideal to use with the inhale and exhale:

Let – Go.
O – pen.
I – Am (doing it).
Re – lax.
Thank – You.
Be – Here.
Ba – by.
Sat – Nam. (traditional mantra, meaning "Truth is All" or "Truth is my Identity")
Jay – Ma. (devotional salutation to the Great Mother)

Ocean Breath (for pregnancy only)

This is an actual technique but not applicable to labor. In labor, you don't want to restrict your breath to inhaling and exhaling through the nose as it is done with this technique. Women in labor exhale frequently through the mouth, often quite vocally. Ocean Breath refers to the yoga breathing technique of ujjayi, or "victorious breath". It is often called Ocean Breath because it generates a sound reminiscent of the sound of the ocean.

To learn the technique, inhale through the nose, and exhale through the mouth uttering a "hhhaaa" sound as if trying to fog a mirror. Inhale again through the nose, but this time exhale through the nose, repeating the "hhhaaa" sound while you keep your mouth closed. You will hear the characteristic sound of ujjayi breathing (ocean sound). Once you are comfortable practicing ujjayi on the exhale, practice with the inhale as well. Keep the inhale and exhale even, without strain or effort. Focus on the sound of the breath, and let the mind relax into the soothing nature of this breath.

I Love You Breath (for pregnancy only)

Pregnant women often find it difficult to take a deep breath when their bellies get bigger. With this breath you can experience a deeper breath as you consciously lengthen and spread your breath throughout the torso. This breath is done in three parts, strengthens the diaphragm and increases lung capacity. Applying Ocean Breath to this technique increases its benefits.

Place one hand on your belly and the other hand on your heart. Take a regular breath and exhale completely. Gently tighten your abdominal muscles to let out as much air as possible. Now begin to inhale into your belly. Imagine that you are filling a cup or water balloon, pouring water into the bottom and slowly all the way to the top. Notice the hand on your belly moving out slightly. Intone silently: "I".

Inhale now into your lungs, ribcage and heart with your breath. Intone silently: "Love".

You have now finished one inhalation. To exhale, slowly start to breathe out from the top down: heart, lungs, ribcage, belly. Imagine you are hugging your baby. Intone silently: "You".

Repeat for ten sets. Do not hold your breath at any point, think of this breath as a smooth wave instead. Transition gently between inhale and exhale, and exhale and inhale.

ASANA PRACTICE

The practice of asana, the third limb of yoga, offers unique benefits for women during pregnancy and labor. I can't even begin to list all the gifts of a regular asana practice for pregnant moms but let me say this: it will improve your overall physical, emotional and mental well-being and likely your experience of labor as well. But these gifts don't come without effort. They are earned through discipline and perseverance. And sometimes they take burning.

Stretching tight muscles can be intense. There are poses I am regularly approaching with a bit of apprehension, even after years of practicing them. Of course, I could skip them or do a half-hearted version (sometimes I do), go through the motions or entertain random thoughts (I frequently do). But while these may be options during asana practice, they are not options during birth (unless you get an epidural). You can't skip contractions, or be half-heartedly in labor. You will have to endure the burning.

Begin with willingness. Remember to let yourself be surprised. When I enter into an intense pose on this premise, I let go of the (dreaded, expected, desired) outcome. Maybe it'll be intense, maybe it won't. This curiosity makes room for focus. I start to pay attention. My breath readily follows suit, wooing my mind to pay greater attention still. As breath and attention deepen, the cells in my body hum along in wakeful presence. On the best days, body and mind are one.

Patanjali, the father of classical yoga, hinges this experience on two fundamental principles: sthira and sukha. In the Yoga Sutras, a two thousand year old collection of aphorisms, the essence of posture is described as "sthira-sukham asanam", meaning that posture (asana) should be equally stable (sthira) and comfortable (sukha). Sthira and sukha are yang and yin, focus and relaxation, firmness and softness, strength and ease.

A yoga pose is done properly when body and mind experience both in equal measure, i.e. when we are fully engaged and at ease at the same time. The breath facilitates this powerful union. The inhalation supports focus and strength; the exhalation brings comfort and ease. But sthira and sukha are not delegated to one aspect of the breath alone. They can be held in each moment.

In labor, your uterus is attempting to do just that. When the upper part of the uterus (fundus) contracts (becomes more firm and hard), the lower part of the uterus (including the cervix) relaxes and softens. This is sthira-sukha in action.

Asana practice provides us with an opportunity to observe and harmonize the interplay of those dynamics. Asana practice also increases our capacity to tolerate stress and discomfort, and helps us accept (and embrace) limitations without resigning. When we practice on the mat, we quickly realize that there is a lot we can't do. There are many poses that require a flexibility or strength we don't have. And even when we get better at some postures, there are always others we are not ready for. But whether we can do certain poses or not, we can always be present with our inner dialog and breathe. It is this presence that beckons us to keep moving, to start over, to not give up.

A few words of caution before you begin: Ensure that the room you practice in is comfortably warm and your stomach mostly empty. Begin with a brief centering followed by a warm-up, and give yourself five minutes or more at the end of your practice for relaxation (suggestions follow). When practicing standing poses or deep stretches, make sure you engage your weight-bearing and stretching muscles to avoid injury. This is especially important toward the end of pregnancy. In your third trimester the pregnancy hormone relaxin will start to soften your pelvic ligaments and joints. To engage your muscles, contract them around your bones and draw energy from the periphery to the mid-line of the body. Ground firmly through any parts of your body that are in touch with the floor. *Consult with your doctor if you have any pre-existing medical conditions to ensure the safety of you and your baby during this practice. Ideally, work with a trained prenatal yoga instructor who understands the anatomy and physiology of pregnancy.*

The following pages outline a twenty minute yoga sequence you can practice at home. Each pose comes with basic alignment instructions and a short (optional) meditation you can reflect on while you practice. Enjoy.

Centering

Sit on a folded blanket with your legs crossed so that your hips are about two to four inches higher than your knees. Elevate your hips as needed. Keep your spine comfortably straight, your shoulders relaxed, and your head balanced atop your shoulders. Tuck your chin slightly and place your hands on your growing belly.

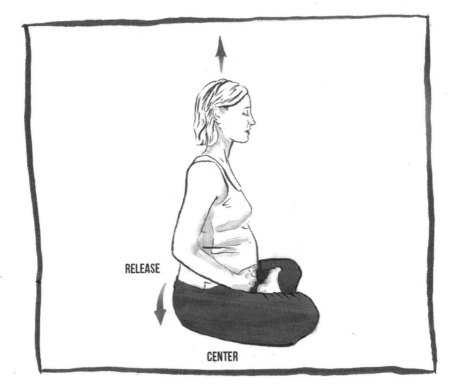

Meditation

I am still as a mountain. Enough within myself.

The mountain doesn't move. It doesn't bemoan the weight it bears.

I breathe into my weight and let my being-ness be enough.

Cat-Cow

Come to your hands and knees. If you are farther along in your pregnancy, separate your knees a bit wider than your hips to make room for your belly. On your inhale, lengthen through the sitting bones and the crown of the head. On your exhale, round your back, flex your head to the chest, and extend your tailbone to the ground. Repeat.

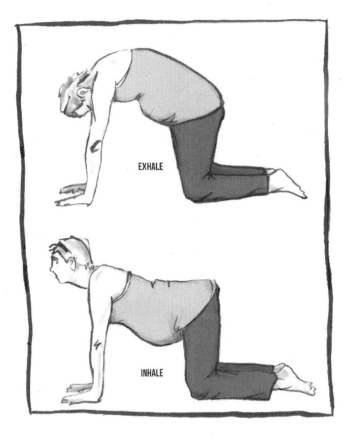

EXHALE

INHALE

Meditation

I breathe with the ocean tide. Rising and falling in continuous succession the wave of my spine.

The circle closes.

Side stretch

On your inhale, reach your right arm overhead, and bend gently to the left as you exhale. Ground through your tail and right sitting bone. Draw your navel back toward your sacrum as if hugging your baby in the womb. Lengthen evenly through both sides of the rib cage. Breathe. Inhale back to center, and repeat on the second side.

Meditation

    I am a vessel on solid ground.

    My own anchor. I cannot fall. I cannot fail as I reach for the stars.

    The sky is the limit.

Downward Dog

From hands and knees, set your hands about seven inches in front of your shoulders. Ground firmly through the first digits of all ten fingers. Tuck your toes under. Lift your knees off the ground as you exhale. Press your hands and feet toward the midline of your body and into the floor. Reach back through the sitting bones. Broaden your shoulders. Relax your head and neck. *Caution: If you are more than 34 weeks along or your baby is in breech position, stay for a shorter time or avoid this pose altogether.*

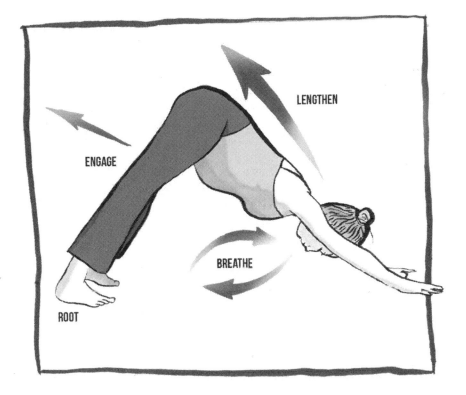

Meditation

My body is a temple; strong and firmly planted are its pillars.

High reaches my navel's dome.

My breath is my worship.

Warrior 1

From Downward Dog, walk your hands back toward your feet. (This is easier than stepping forward if you are farther along in your pregnancy.) Slowly roll up to standing as you keep your arms and torso relaxed.

Step your right leg forward about two feet. Exhale and bend your right knee, centering it directly above or slightly behind the ankle. With your back heel lifted, release your sacrum and tail bone to the ground. Inhale to lift your arms overhead. To switch sides, step your left leg forward to meet the right. Step your right leg back and repeat on the second side. When done, place both hands on the ground and return to Downward Dog. Breathe.

Meditation

I am held in the bowl of my pelvis. Not a part of me is lost.

I am here. Fully in my center. Don't you see?

Warrior 2

From Downward Dog, walk your hands back toward your feet. Slowly roll up to standing as you keep your arms and torso relaxed. Step your right leg forward about two feet. Place your left heel at a 45 degree angle onto the ground. Exhale and bend your right knee, centering it directly above or slightly behind the ankle. Rotate your hips, belly and chest a quarter turn to the left while keeping your front knee centered above the ankle. Engage your pelvic floor to support the weight of your growing belly.

On your next inhale, extend your arms out to the side. Turn your gaze to the front. To switch sides, step your left leg forward to meet the right leg. Step your right leg back and repeat on the second side. When done, place both hands on the ground and come to sitting. Breathe.

Meditation

    I have arrived. I am where I need to be.

    The past is my resource as I step into the future. My gaze is my aim.

    I am ready.

Seated Wide Angle

Sit with your legs out to the side. Support your hips with a folded blanket to sit comfortably with your spine lifted. Ground through the backs of your legs and draw them into the pelvis. Press through your sitting bones. You can add a round of Kegel exercises to this practice (squeeze your pelvic floor muscles on the exhale, release on the inhale, or hold for a few breaths before releasing).

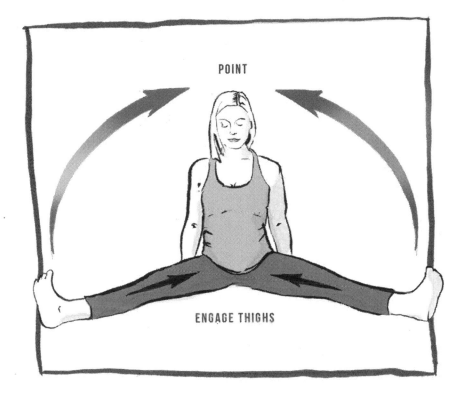

Meditation

I am radiant Mother Earth.

My pelvis is my throne, my sitting bones the gate of birth.

I am vast and spacious.

Seated twist

Come to a comfortable seated position. You can kneel on your heels, or sit cross-legged and place one foot over the opposite leg. Keep both sitting bones in contact with the floor. Engage your abdominal muscles and pelvic floor. Inhale and lift through your spine. On your exhale, gently twist through the *mid and upper back*. Avoid twisting below the diaphragm to keep the womb environment stable. Repeat on the other side.

Meditation

Coming from a place of seeing, I reach for the unseen.

Winding and unwinding along the spiral staircase of my spine.

I breathe and pause at each step.

There is no rush.

Supported Child's pose

Kneeling on a carpet or firm mattress, place a large firm pillow between your legs to support the weight of your hips and belly. Arrange a big pile of firmly folded blankets and pillows in front of you. Lean forward to rest on your props with your heart higher than your hips. Make sure you feel very comfortable.

Meditation

I am small, the earth is my cradle.

It is all I need to know.

I am.

Side-lying relaxation pose

Sit on a blanket or firm mattress, and lower yourself onto your side with your knees bent. Rest your head on a pillow or folded blanket, and place a pillow or yoga bolster between your knees. Use additional folded blankets to support your belly and to rest your arm.

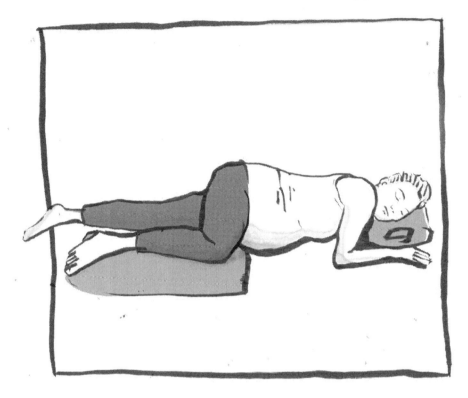

Meditation

I am infinite, the sky is my womb.

It is all I need to know.

I am.

TODAY

As we say good-bye to each other, I want to thank you for coming here and meeting up with me. I've been waiting for this. I've been counting the days and months to get here, to arrive at today. It snowed the day before, an unusual occurrence where I live, stopping traffic, closing schools and businesses, slowing down time. Yesterday's snow, the strong winds the day before, the heavy rain the weeks prior, all has become part of today. So too has all that you've read in this book, all you've dreamed about and have ever experienced become part of you. Today you are all you could ever be. Today is yours.

Eventually, today will become the day of your baby's birth. What of today will be memorable, will flow into your labor like a stream into a river? What have you been waiting for?

Make today your prayer and your thanksgiving. Don't miss a beat of its sacred pulse. Breathe its transient blessing, and remember to love. Here is a parent prayer I share at the closing of the last Yoga Way to Birth class. Parents sit back to back with each other in meditation during this time. You can do the same with your partner when contractions first start and read the prayer together, bowing to the work about to begin.

As I sit here with you, my child, I am filled with joy and longing.
Before you were conceived, I wanted you,
before I felt you move for the first time, I knew you,
and I loved you before you readied yourself to be born.

You are a love song etched into my soul, and I promise to listen with
every breath as you pluck the strings of my heart to
announce your arrival and presence.
I promise to be a good parent,
looking out for your safety and wellbeing,
trusting the unfolding of your journey, and
embracing every step we take along the way together.
May your life be filled with light.

Acknowledgements

Thank you to all who have helped me birth this book. Emory, for your exquisite edits, for your admiration, cheerleading and excellency as a teacher and friend. Deah, for conceiving, gestating, birthing and nursing the Yoga Way to Birth with me into its toddler years. Without you this book wouldn't exist. I bow to you, dear friend.

Thank you, Maria, for gifting me with the yoga book that led me into my first yoga class. Tina K, Sarahjoy, Matt and Anne, thank you for introducing me to asana practice, breath, meditation, alignment, Patanjali, and Krishna Das. Thank you, DaeJa, for guiding me onto the Buddhist path and for blessing me like a sweet child at the end of a retreat. I needed this blessing.

Vande gurunam, Casey. Thank you for your service to Near East Yoga and Guruji's lineage, for your humility, gentleness, steadfastness, your awesome (physical and mental) adjustments, and for knowing how to explain the inexplicable. You are a rock star.

Heartfelt thanks to the Portland midwives, doulas, prenatal yoga teachers and communities who have supported the Yoga Way to Birth classes with referrals over the years. Special thanks to Laura Erickson for giving our classes its first home at Alma Midwifery, and to Shana for your friendship and consistent support.

I am deeply grateful to all the parents who have searched and found the Yoga Way to Birth and taken our classes. Your questions and comments have helped polish our curriculum; your quest for self-knowledge has been my delight.

Thank you, Gabe, for nailing the design for this book (as you have nailed every other single design in the past). It was worth the wait!

Finally, I thank you Felix, and Hanna, and Saskia for coming into my life. You have been an inspiration for me from the day you were born. I am proud of you and deeply gratified to see that you are taking up the path of yoga for yourself, now that you are on your way to adulthood and making your own decisions. Jai ma!

And Mark, thank you, Love. Thank you for helping me with book formatting, edits, the dishes, money, time, for your brilliant thoughts, for always being present with me regardless the hour of the day (or night) and, above all, for never giving up on me.

Appendix

Glossary

Common Labor Terms

Amniotic Fluid: This protective liquid, consisting mostly of water, fills in the sac surrounding the fetus.

APGAR: A measurement of the newborn's response to birth and life outside the womb. The ratings, APGAR, are based on Appearance (color), Pulse (heartbeat), Grimace (reflex), Activity (muscle tone), and Respiration (breathing). The scores, which are taken at 1 and 5 minutes following birth, range from 10 to 1, with 10 being the highest and 1 being the lowest.

Breech Presentation: Where the fetus is positioned head up to be born buttocks first or with one or both feet first. This occurs in less than five percent of all births.

Cesarean Section: An incision through the abdominal and uterine walls for extraction of the fetus; it may be vertical or, more commonly, horizontal. Also called abdominal delivery; commonly called C-Section.

Colostrum: Baby's first food, this is a cream-colored fluid discharged from the breasts at the beginning of milk production, and usually noticeable during the last couple of weeks of pregnancy.

Contraction: The regular tightening of the uterus, working to dilate and efface the cervix and to push the baby down the birth canal.

Crowned/Crowning: The baby's head is emerging at the vaginal opening and about to be born.

Dilation: The extent to which the cervix has opened in preparation for childbirth. It is measured in centimeters, with full dilation being 10 centimeters.

Effacement: This refers to the thinning of the cervix in preparation for birth, and is expressed in percentages. You'll be 100% effaced when you begin pushing.

Engaged: The baby's presenting part (usually the head) has settled into the pelvic cavity, which usually happens during the last month of pregnancy.

Epidural: A common method of administering anesthesia during labor. It is inserted through a catheter threaded through a needle inserted into the dura space near the spinal cord.

Episiotomy: An incision made during childbirth to the perineum, the muscle between the vagina and rectum, to widen the vaginal opening for an emergency delivery.

4-1-1: This refers to a useful mnemonic device that indicates that active labor has probably started. When the contractions are 4 minutes apart, last 1 minute and have been that way for about 1 hour, it is a good time to settle into your birth place.

Fetal Distress: Condition when the baby is not receiving enough oxygen or is experiencing some other complication.

Fontanelle: Soft spots between the unfused sections of the baby's skull. These allow the baby's head to compress slightly during passage through the birth canal.

Forceps: Tong like instruments which may be used to help guide the baby's head out of the birth canal during delivery.

Induced Labor: Labor is started or accelerated through intervention, such as placing prostaglandin gel on the cervix, using an IV drip of the synthetic version of the hormone oxytocin (Pitocin), or by rupturing the amniotic membranes.

Labor: Regular contractions of the uterus that result in dilation and effacement of the cervix.

Lightening: When the baby drops into the mother's pelvis in preparation for delivery (See Engaged).

Meconium: Baby's first bowel movement, this is the greenish-black substance that builds up in the bowels of a growing fetus and is normally discharged shortly after birth.

Oxytocin: Hormone secreted by the pituitary gland that stimulates contractions and the milk-eject reflex. Pitocin is the synthetic form of this hormone.

Perineum: The muscle and tissue between the vagina and the rectum.

Perineal Massage: The gentle stretching and massaging of the skin between the anus and vagina (perineum) during the last few weeks of pregnancy with the goal of reducing the incidence of episiotomy and perineal tears during birth.

Pitocin: A synthetic form of the naturally occurring hormone oxytocin, often administered to induce or augment slow labor.

Placenta: The organ which connects the mother and fetus that transports nourishment and takes away waste.

Placenta Previa: When the placenta partially covers the opening of the uterus.

Posterior: The baby is in a face-up position during delivery. Normal presentation is anterior, which is face down.

Postpartum: The period after childbirth

Post-Term: Pregnancy lasting beyond 42 weeks.

Preterm: Babies born earlier than 37 weeks.

Ruptured Membranes: Usually refers to the breaking of the fluid filled sac surrounding the baby. The fluid may come as a gush of water or as a slow leak. Slow leaks are sometimes mistaken as incontinence.

Station: Describes how far the baby has descended into the mother's pelvis. Station is measured by the relationship of the fetal head to the ischial spines, and ranges from -4 (baby floating above the ischial spines) to +4 (baby is crowning). When baby reaches 0 station it is said to be engaged in the pelvis.

Timing Contractions: Contractions are measured from the beginning of one contraction until the beginning of the next. It is useful to time contractions for a short duration to assess the status of labor, primarily whether the shift to active labor has occurred. It is not necessary to time contractions throughout labor.

Transition: This refers to the last part of active labor – when your cervix dilates from 8 to a full 10 centimeters. It marks the shift to the second stage of labor. This can be the most intense part of labor. Contractions are usually very strong, coming more frequently two and lasting a minute or more, and you may start shaking and shivering.

Transverse: Baby's body length is horizontal in the uterus. If the baby cannot be moved, it will have to be delivered by cesarean section.

Umbilical Cord: The cord that carries blood, oxygen and nutrients to the baby from the placenta during pregnancy, and carries waste from the baby to be disposed by the mother's body.

FURTHER READING

Caring for Yourself in Pregnancy and Birth

Buckley, S. J. (2008). *Gentle Birth, Gentle Mothering*. Berkeley, CA: Celestial Arts.

England, P., & Horowitz, R. (1998). *Birthing from Within*. Albuquerque, NM: Partera Press.

Simkin, P. (1989). *The Birth Partner*. Boston, MA: The Harvard Common Press.

St. John, R. (2008). *Fathers at Birth*. Ringing Bell Press.

Gaskin, I. M. (2003). *Ina May's Guide to Childbirth*. New York, NY: Bantam Dell.

Lasater, J. (1995). *Relax and Renew*. Berkeley, CA: Rodmell Press.

Davis-Floyd, R. E. (2003). *Birth as an American Rite of Passage*. Berkeley, CA: University of California Press.

Dick-Read, G. (2004). *Childbirth without Fear: The Principles and Practices of Natural Childbirth*. London: Pinter and Martin Ltd.

Yoga and Meditation

Desikachar, T.K.V. (1999). *The Heart of Yoga*. Rochester, VT: Inner Traditions International.

Maharaji, Sri N. (2011). *I Am That*. Durham, NC: The Acorn Press.

Rinpoche, Y. M. (2007). *The Joy of Living*. New York, NY: Three Rivers Press.

Brach, T. (2003). *Radical Acceptance*. New York, NY: Bantam Dell.

Nhat Hanh, T. (1987). *The Miracle of Mindfulness*. Boston, MA: Beacon Press.

Bolte Taylor, J. (2006). *My Stroke of Insight*. New York, NY: Penguin Group.

Rinpoche, K. (2008). *This Precious Life*. Boston, MA: Shambala.

Ray, R. A. (2008). *Touching Enlightenment: Finding Realization in the Body*. Boulder, CO: Sounds True.

Yogananda, P. (2007). *Scientific Healing Affirmations*. Los Angeles, CA: Self-Realization Fellowship.

Rahula, W. (1974). *What the Buddha Taught*. New York, NY: Grove Press.

Epstein, M. (2002). *Going on Being*. New York, NY: Broadway Books.

Iyengar, B.K.S. (2002). *The Tree of Yoga*. Boston, MA: Shambala Classics.

Yoga for Birth

Balaskas, J. (2003). *Preparing for Birth with Yoga*. London: Harper Collins Publishing.

Kaur Khalsa, G. (2003). *Bountiful, Beautiful, Blissful*. New York, NY: Saint Martins Press.

Gates, J. (2006). *Yogini: The Power of Women in Yoga*. San Rafael, CA: Mandala Publishing.

Bardacke, N. (2012). *Mindful Birthing: Training the Mind, Body, and Heart for Childbirth and Beyond*. New York, NY: Harper Collins Publishing.

The Wonderful Female Body

Northrup, C. (2010). *Women's Bodies, Women's Wisdom*. New York, NY: Bantam Books.

Kent, T. L. (2008). *Wild Feminine*. Portland, OR: Tami Lynn Kent

Calais-Germain, B. (2003). *The Female Pelvis*. Seattle, WA: Eastland Press.

About the Author

Tina Lilly is a certified yoga instructor, childbirth educator and licensed professional counselor in private practice. She has trained as a labor doula and attended births. As the co-founder and lead instructor of the Yoga Way to Birth, she trains prenatal yoga instructor, doulas, childbirth educators and other birth professionals in mindfulness-based approaches to client and self care. She also offers certification trainings for individuals interested in teaching the Yoga Way to Birth in their communities.

For questions or more information, please contact the author.

WWW.YOGAWAYTOBIRTH.COM

Made in the USA
San Bernardino, CA
14 July 2017